In Search of the
Northern
Saints

by Simon Webb

New Revised and Enlarged Edition

Foreword by the Bishop of Jarrow

The cover shows a detail of The Death of St Oswald, from British Library Royal Manuscript B VII (C14th)

This book is dedicated to the memory of King Sigeberht of the East Angles: bravest of them all

CONTENTS

A sick man is cured by St Cuthbert's girdle:
from British Library Yates Thompson
manuscript 26, C12th

Foreword

As I read this book I found myself asking time and time again what it was about these saints that made them so remarkable, so that long after they were dead people still talked about them and revered them and in some cases cared for their bodies. There must have been something that made them stand out from the other people amongst whom they were living.

For me the story of St Aidan seems to give a good clue as to why these people were remembered – and are still remembered today. One of the most famous stories that Bede tells of Aidan is that of King Oswin giving Aidan a horse to help him in his travels. Almost immediately Aidan meets a man begging for alms and he gives him his horse with all its royal trappings to sell, without any concern for the fact that he will now have to continue to walk everywhere.

There was clearly a reckless generosity about Aidan which people found deeply attractive and which seems to have sprung out of his devotion to the God whom he sought to serve. Time and time again over the centuries we see how deeply attractive are those who live their lives with a spirit of generosity. In the twentieth century we saw it in the life of a man like Maximillian Kolbe who was willing to give up his own life to save the life of a young Polish father in the death camp. In our own century we see it in the life and death of the seven peacemakers of the Melanesian Brotherhood* who were willing to do anything to try to bring peace to their country.

We might reflect that our world needs that sense of radical generosity more than ever. There is much around us that seeks to encourage us to be less than generous in our attitude to others; to think the worst rather than the best of people; to seek constantly to doubt people's motives; to pillory those whose lives encounter difficulties and often sadly to be less than generous in our attitude to those who for whatever reason are most vulnerable and in need in our society. Some of this seems sadly to be motivated by a need to show that somehow we are better than other people. Aidan and Oswin and other of the saints mentioned in this book seem to have had little concern about proving that they were better than others. Their concern seems rather to have been to provide for those most in need and for Cuthbert that included the natural world. In the story that Bede tells of the eagle that provides fish for the saint and his companion to eat, Cuthbert is insistent that the eagle must have half of the fish. It is almost as if that generosity of spirit which we need so much today runs through the very veins of the saints depicted in this book.

This generosity leads naturally to a deep valuing of every human being. After Aidan has given away his horse, King Oswin, understandably remonstrates with him and Aidan turns and asks him "What are you saying, Your Majesty? Is this child of a mare more valuable to you than this child of God?" Michael Ramsey, Bishop of Durham (1952-56) said of Aidan "It was not by cleverness or by eloquence but by a very simply love for human souls, born of a love for Christ, that Aidan conquered". The vision that every single human being is a "child of God" and worthy of every respect and human dignity is again something that we in our part of the twenty-first century need to hear again. In a world where individuals can too easily be discarded as just another statistic and where people who we think different from us can be too easily held up to ridicule we need to hear again Aidan talking to us of "this child of God".

Simon writes towards the end of this book, "The twelve northern saints who dominate this book all lived during times of great change, when important decisions had to be made about the future direction of Britain and the various ethnic groups who lived on these islands". Readers of this book may feel that those challenges are ours too today. If we are, in the midst of all the challenges that face us, to make our country and our world a place that is good and godly and human for everybody and where the natural world is treated with the respect that it both deserves and needs, we may find that these northern saints have much to teach us.

Mark Bryant, Bishop of Jarrow

Feast of Maximillian Kolbe 2009

*To learn more of the death and life of the seven peacemakers of the Melanesian Mission read *In Search of the Lost* by Richard Anthony Carter. (Canterbury Press, 2006).

I. Edix Hill

The Pagan Anglo-Saxons; St Augustine; Bede

Some time in the seventh century AD, a young Anglo-Saxon woman was buried at Edix Hill in Cambridgeshire, and into her pagan grave was placed a fossilised sea-urchin. Although some types of stone teem with such fossils, these represent only a tiny fraction of the millions of living things that once lived in the ancient seas. The woman buried with the stone shellfish is, likewise, one of the very few Anglo-Saxons who remained in the memory of the soil long enough to be discovered in modern times.

We have no idea why the fossil was buried with the woman. It is possible that the people of the time knew it had once been a living sea-urchin, but they could not have understood the process of fossilisation that had turned it to stone. Traditionally, these fossils have been regarded as the hearts of petrified children, as 'fairy bread', the 'crown of the shepherds' or a charm to keep milk fresh, among other things. In the Christian world some people used to believe that these fossils, with their star-shaped decoration, marked the route taken by the Wise Men as they followed the star to Bethlehem. Why the Wise Men would have taken a detour through Cambridgeshire on their journey to Bethlehem is another question.

The grave of the Edix Hill woman was unusually rich in grave-goods, even for a pagan Anglo-Saxon burial. The occupant of the grave, who was probably between seventeen and twenty-five years old when she died, was laid out on a proper wooden bed, and surrounded by such items as weaving equipment, silver rings, a knife, a key, and the curious little fossil.

The fact that this lady was buried with such care and attention seems especially surprising when we learn that she had been suffering from a very bad case of leprosy. In her last days of life, she would have looked quite pitiful – she had lost several teeth, her face would have been covered with raised nodules and there would have been a steady discharge of fluid from her nose.

In later times, European lepers were often cast out of communities and forced to live the life of roving beggars, or obliged to live quarantined in leper-houses, even though leprosy is not very infectious. But the pagan friends and relatives of the Edix Hill woman had taken the time and trouble to give her a humane and compassionate burial. There is no suggestion that this woman was not regarded as anything other than a respected member of the community, right up until her early death. Given her age, and the severity of her disease, it seems unlikely that she had ever been married. In many ancient societies (and too many modern ones) unmarried women have extremely low status; but the Edix Hill woman was buried like a queen.

Christian historians have sometimes depicted the ancient pagans of Britain as a savage people, living in a kind of ignorant darkness before the light of Christianity came upon them. Those who buried the Edix Hill woman come across as pretty enlightened – especially when one considers that this leprous woman might have been treated far worse in a later, Christian society.

Leprosy is frequently mentioned in the both the Old and New Testaments, and for Christians in Europe its appearance among their own people must have been a reminder that they lived in a world similar to that depicted in the Bible. The Edix Hill woman and her pagan friends, however, were probably quite ignorant of the Bible, where leprosy is often depicted as a terrible curse, although modern commentators believe that the word translated as 'leprosy' in, for instance, the King James Bible of the seventeenth century, probably referred to a wide range of skin complaints.

Burials such as those at Edix Hill are a long, narrow window into the early Anglo-Saxon period, about which we know surprisingly little. The Anglo-Saxons are known to be the ancestors of many people living in England today, but because most of these ancestors were illiterate, and built their houses out of perishable materials, much about their lives is still a mystery.

The damp, fertile soil of England is usually not as kind to historic remains as the dry soil of Egypt, where even extremely delicate items such as pieces of cloth, leather and papyrus are sometimes well-preserved. Even where archaeologists know that Anglo-Saxon remains might be found at a particular site, they are often frustrated by the fact that, over hundreds of years, new buildings have been put up on top of anything that the early Anglo-Saxons may have left behind.

We know a surprising amount about the Romans in Britain, who built in stone and wrote and read in Latin. But for decades after the Romans abandoned Britain around 410AD, the evidence of how the people lived is scarce; so scarce that the term 'Dark Age' is appropriate, not because it refers to a pagan time, but to a mysterious time.

One date for the end of Dark Age England is that of the landing of St Augustine of Canterbury, the so-called Apostle of the English, at Thanet in the year 597. Augustine brought an advanced form of literacy, and the possibility of a more detailed record of history, back into England.

The first historians of Britain are all put in the shade by the achievement of a humble monk from an out-of-the-way little place called Jarrow. Some time during the first half of the eighth century AD, the Venerable Bede set himself the task of writing the church history of the English people. When he had finished re-telling the old stories he had learned from earlier writers, he began to write about people who lived nearer to his own time. If we think of this period as a geological level in a cliff-face, we can see Bede's *Ecclesiastical History* as a geologist's hammer, chipping away until the best fossils are revealed. Of these, the most fascinating examples include twelve remarkable northern saints.

II. Durham

Oswald and Cuthbert

As a Christian, Saint Oswald of Northumbria would not have expected a burial such as that given to the young woman found at Edix Hill, with its many valuable grave-goods: Christian graves tend to contain little more than bones. As a king, Oswald might, however, have expected to be housed for eternity under rather better conditions than those in which he sleeps today. The sad fact is that the royal skull is stored separately from the rest of the body, and the whereabouts of the rest cannot be established with any certainty. St Oswald's skull also shares someone else's tomb with the bones of other people. What is worse, this tomb has been disturbed several times over the centuries.

Oswald might take comfort from the fact that the people with whom he shares the tomb in question are also saints, including the famous St Cuthbert, whose tomb it is. And the tomb itself lies under the flagstones of Durham Cathedral – one of the oldest and most magnificent cathedrals in Europe.

When the tomb was opened in 1899, a Dr Selby W. Plummer was able to examine the various bones that had lain inside for over a thousand years. These included the head of Oswald, who had been killed in battle when Cuthbert was about eight years old. Selby Plummer's investigation of Oswald's skull produced some startling findings.

Cuthbert's tomb had already been opened earlier in the nineteenth century, in 1827. This investigation was led by James Raine, a canon of the cathedral and an amateur local historian. Raine was just one of the many Anglican priests of the eighteenth and nineteenth centuries who occupied themselves with various branches of knowledge, ranging from bee-keeping to the study of ancient standing-stones. In the language of the times, Raine was an antiquary, and the opening of Cuthbert's tomb was an opportunity for him to combine his profession of priest with his passion for history.

The 1827 opening took place against the background of changes to the status of Roman Catholics in England – changes that eventually led to the Catholic Relief Act of 1829. In the 1820s, in Durham itself, a new Catholic church was being built on Old Elvet, almost within sight of the Cathedral. Such developments caused real panic in the minds of some narrow-minded Anglicans: would reform change the balance of power between the Church of England and the Roman

Catholic Church in the British Isles?

Raine's explorations were partly motivated by his desire to scotch a story that had been going around in Catholic circles since the Reformation – that St Cuthbert was not in fact buried in his supposed tomb inside Durham Cathedral. The Catholics claimed that his real body had been spirited away and buried elsewhere, in a secret place known only to three Catholic monks at any one time. If Raine could find a shred of proof that the tomb really did contain the genuine body of Cuthbert, that would be one in the eye for the Catholic doubters.

Given Raine's rather careless approach, his limited skills as a draughtsman and the primitive state of archaeology at the time, it was inevitable that he would not be able to prove conclusively that the skeleton in the tomb was Cuthbert's. He practically ignored Oswald's skull altogether.

Selby Plummer and the other investigators of 1899 were not really concerned with the authenticity or otherwise of the main Durham skeleton. Their reason for opening the tomb was to get hold of the last pieces of an ancient wooden coffin that Raine's team had partially recovered seventy-two years earlier. The chance to examine and even photograph anything else that remained inside the tomb was a bonus.

When the cover-stone was lifted off in 1899, the replacement coffin that Raine had installed to house the bones was revealed. This shoddy bone-crate fell apart as soon as it was lifted, and the bones inside were all jumbled together.

It seems that, with the exception of a shot of the gaping mouth of the tomb, the photographs from 1899 haven't survived; but carefully-proportioned drawings made from the photos were reproduced with Selby Plummer's report. The drawings of Oswald's skull are clearly based on a photograph taken when the skull had been assembled, like a three-dimensional jigsaw, from its component parts.

Most of the skull above the level of the cheek-bones had been broken into pieces, some of them several inches long. The size of the pieces ruled out the possibility that the skull had been damaged long after death, by which time the bone would have become dry and brittle, and would have shattered into many smaller pieces. The skull, it seems, had been damaged, but not during its long rest in Cuthbert's tomb. The damage had happened during life, and had caused the death of the saint.

III. The River Idle

Oswald and Edwin

Today, most English first-names are derived from Latin or French names, or from English translations of the Bible. The top ten boys' names in 2007 included the old favourites Thomas and James (both Biblical), William (from the French Guillaume) and Daniel and Joshua, which are also Biblical.

This was certainly not the case in Anglo-Saxon England, where the people continued to use non-Biblical, non-Latin names. Many of these now cause great merriment among school-children when they are being taught about the period in primary school. Names like Aethelfrith can act as a real barrier to people trying to take the earliest English seriously. The Anglo-Saxon name problem is further complicated by the fact that in those days many people shared similar names. As well as Oswald's father Aethelfrith, there were also Aethelbald, Aethelberht, Aethelburh, Aethelheard, and at least ten other important historical characters, both male and female, whose names started with 'Aethel'.

Aethelfrith, who was killed around 616 AD, was the father of Oswald, king and saint of Northumbria. He was king of Bernicia, an area conquered by the Angles, which stretched from the Forth to the Tees, and was roughly equivalent to the modern counties of Northumberland, Durham, Berwickshire and East Lothian.

The Angles were just one of several groups of Germanic invaders who began to occupy what we now call England from around the fifth century AD. These groups, which also included the Jutes and of course the Saxons, are now lumped under the term 'Anglo-Saxons', but Bede insists that it was the Angles alone who settled in what he calls Northumbria.

In modern times, there has been some disagreement among historians about whether the Anglo-Saxons used violence to sweep the indigenous Celtic population into the West, or whether these newcomers were peaceful settlers who lived alongside the Celtic natives. Two recent DNA surveys which might have settled the question contradicted each other, but written sources from the period, together with place-names, and evidence locked inside the English language itself, seem to give a lot of weight to the old idea of a warlike invasion.

The old histories tell us that Anglo-Saxon warriors were originally invited into Britain to fight as mercenaries against the Picts, and also the Scots (meaning the Irish) of the North. Soon they came in such numbers that their homelands over the sea were quite empty of people. They then started to gain the upper hand in their new country.

The character of Oswald's father Aethelfrith shows definite signs of his warrior ancestry. His name means 'noble peace', but it was by no means a name he lived up to. According to Bede, Aethelfrith ruled Bernicia for twenty-four years, during which time he conquered so much land and killed so many people that Bede compared him to Benjamin in the Biblical book of Genesis. Of Benjamin it was said that he would 'ravin as a wolf'. One of Aethelfrith's achievements was to annex the neighbouring kingdom of Deira, which lay to the south of Bernicia, in 604.

Aethelfrith was a pagan by religion, but many of the people he fought against were Christians. These included the Brythonic people, or Britons, the Celtic race whom the Anglo-Saxons were forcing further and further west as they gobbled up their land. Pagan though he was, Aethelfrith, King of Bernicia, recognised the potential power of the Christian God. In a battle near Chester, he noticed a body of unarmed men on the British side, who turned out to be monks from Bangor Iscoed, in what is now the modern Welsh county of Gwynedd. Since they were there to pray for a British victory, Aethelfrith slaughtered almost all of them – supposedly twelve hundred men.

The story of how Aethelfrith met his own end is also the story of how his son Oswald started to put together the pieces that were later to make him such a remarkable ruler in his own right. Aethelfrith had forced a Deiran prince called Edwin into exile, during which exile he found shelter at the court of Readwald, King of the East Angles. This Readwald is still regarded by some as the king who was given an elaborate ship burial at Sutton Hoo in East Anglia, and who might therefore have been the owner of the famous Sutton Hoo masked helmet. The burial at Sutton Hoo had both pagan and Christian features, and this is consistent with what we know about Readwald from the written sources. Though technically a Christian, Readwald hedged his bets by setting up a pagan altar alongside his Christian one.

Aethelfrith tried to reach out his arm across the intervening kingdom of Lindsey, south of the Humber, to have Edwin killed, despite the fact that Edwin was his own brother-in-law (brother of his second wife, Acha). He attempted to bribe Readwald to murder the exile, but the East-Anglian king refused. At last, Readwald met Aethelfrith in battle near the River Idle, probably at Bawtry, to the south-east of Doncaster. Readwald was victorious, and Aethelfrith was killed. Soon Edwin himself was King of Northumbria, the new kingdom forged out of the combination of Bernicia and Deira.

Oswald, son of Aethelfrith, must have been about twelve at this time, and would suddenly have found the ruling dynasty of which he was a member falling about his ears. It was time for him to go into exile, as his father's enemy Edwin had done.

The story of Edwin's victory over Aethelfrith has many features that are typical of English politics in Anglo-Saxon times. First, there is the existence of many kingdoms on what we now think of as English soil; kingdoms that were constantly either fighting each other, forming alliances or sheltering exiles from other kingdoms. These kingdoms did not have borders in the modern sense, and changed in size and shape according to the military and political fortunes of their rulers.

There is also the existence at the same time, but in different areas, of Christians and pagans, and the fact that the religion of an area seemed to follow the religion of its king. Aethelfrith's fall also shows us how the fate of a kingdom could depend on the success of its king – if the king was killed, his administration would usually fall and his kingdom would be taken over by his nemesis. Another typical feature of the fall of Aethelfrith is the fact that the man who brought him down was a close relative.

Readwald's rapid advance on Aethelfrith recalls another feature of Anglo-Saxon life. Readwald probably marched his men up a Roman road; a reminder that the people of his time lived among the remains of a Roman occupation that had only ended some two hundred years before. For at least part of his route, Readwald must have taken the Roman road now called Ermine Street, which connected such important Roman cities as Lindum (modern Lincoln) and Eboracum (York).

IV. Rome

Gregory the Great, Paulinus and Augustine

Like monarchies throughout history, the Northumbrian kings attempted to form alliances by marriage. Edwin married the Kentish princess Aethelburh, whose people had been Christians for some time. Edwin's bride brought with her from Kent a newly-consecrated bishop called Paulinus, one of the 'second wave' of missionaries sent to England by Pope Gregory I, four years after Saint Augustine first landed in 597.

This book is about twelve saints of northern Britain, but it would not be complete without some details on a sixth saint, Pope Gregory I, known as the Great.

Gregory never came to Britain, though, as we shall see, he once attempted to make the journey. He was born into a wealthy and aristocratic family in Rome around 540 AD. He was extremely well-educated, and in the earlier, pagan Rome of the Emperor Augustus he would probably have been destined for a career in the army, or politics, or both. But Gregory abandoned his chances of success outside the Church and turned his large house on Rome's Caelian Hill into a monastery; St Andrew's. There he lived as a monk and enjoyed what he later looked back on as the happiest period of his life.

Gregory seems to have been the kind of man who gives off a very confident and capable vibe, even at a very early age. In his thirties he was made a deacon, and at the age of thirty-nine he was chosen by the then Pope to be papal ambassador to the court of the Roman Emperor. This was a very important job, as Gregory was expected to liaise between the Pope in Rome, and the Emperor, who by that time had his headquarters not in Rome but at Constantinople.

Although the Roman Empire in the west collapsed in the fifth century AD, the eastern empire (known as the Byzantine Empire because Constantinople had once been called Byzantium) survived until 1453. But the emperors Tiberius II and Maurice, whom Gregory begged for help, were unable to do much for the Roman homeland of Italy.

When Gregory became pope in 590, Rome was in a terrible state after years of war, plague, floods, drought and general neglect. Despite his own chronic ill-health, the new pope set about reforming the papacy and trying to bring peace and plenty to the people under his control.

As well as affairs at home, Gregory had a keen interest in the state of the Christian church throughout the rest of Europe. He clearly thought it was part of his job as pope to spread the Roman Catholic variety of Christianity, and to eliminate paganism. In the sixth century, paganism, which Gregory sometimes called the worship of 'sticks and stones' was still common, especially on the islands of Sicily and Sardinia, and in the Campania region of the Italian mainland.

In the islands of Britain, which had once been part of the Roman Empire, Gregory knew that the pagan Anglo-Saxons had pushed the Christian Britons into the West. Gregory had a particular interest in converting these new people, whom he would probably have thought of as the Anglii.

The story goes that, some time before he became pope, the saint encountered two blue-eyed, blond-haired, fair-skinned Angles in Rome. When he was told that they were Angles, he disagreed and said they were angels. When they explained that their king was called Aelle, he said he thought they should learn to sing alleluias. When they told him that they belonged to the tribe of the Deiri, he said that they should be allowed to escape the anger of God (*de ira Dei* in Latin).

Some versions of the story say that the Angles were slaves being sold in Rome – others assert that they were ambassadors of some kind.

In his biography of Gregory, Jeffrey Richards doubts that Gregory's first encounter with the Angles would have happened in quite this way, especially since the future pope wasn't given to such whimsical puns. He did have a sense of humour, but it was generally much drier and darker.

We don't know exactly how Gregory first became aware of the Angles, but we do know that he owned English slaves. The slave-trade from the British Isles was another bad side-effect of the frequent wars between the different kingdoms in Britain: if male, able-bodied prisoners were taken, they would either serve their captors as slaves at home, or be exported to the Continent. Female prisoners of war would sometimes end up serving as wives or concubines to their captors.

After his first sight of the angelic-looking Angles (if this really happened) Gregory tried to set off for Britain to convert them, with the permission of the pope. Gregory was, however, so popular with the people of Rome that the pope was forced to call him back. According to the legend, Gregory was able to take this setback philosophically, as he had already had a message from God which seemed to foresee his return to the Eternal City. As he sat reading his Bible, just four days into his journey, a locust settled on the page, and Gregory said in Latin, '*Ecce locusta!*' (look at the locust). The second word reminded him of the Latin phrase '*loco sta*' meaning 'stay in place'.

After he became pope himself, Gregory did not forget the Anglii. In 596 he chose Augustine, the abbot of his monastery of St Andrew, to travel to

Britain with forty monks, to convert the English.

The party got as far as southern Gaul before horror-stories of what lay on the other side of the Channel made them falter. It may be that the Gauls filled their ears with some of the disconcerting notions about Britain then current among people on the continent. The sixth-century Roman writer Procopius related that the fishermen of Armorica (Brittany) spent some of their time ferrying dead souls from the European mainland to these remote, mysterious islands near the edge of the known world. The Breton fisherman would be knocked up in the middle of the night, and compelled to cross the Channel with their ghostly cargo which, although it was invisible, still made their boats ride low in the water. It was said that, because these fishermen performed this useful service and thus rid the Continent of its dead souls, they were exempt from tax.

Augustine went all the way to Rome to beg Gregory to let him abandon his mission, but the pope sent Augustine back. The mission started in Kent, where the local king already had a Christian wife – a Parisian princess called Bertha. The success of the mission encouraged Gregory to send a second wave of monks in 601, among whom was Paulinus.

The strategy of trying to convert a kingdom by converting its ruler first seems to have been the preferred approach of missionaries in pagan England. The advantages of this are obvious – in areas ruled over by what were in effect warlords, any attempt to convert the population from the grass roots up could have been interpreted as some sort of attempt to promote rebellion. If the missionaries attempted a top-down approach, then they might not be seen as a threat to the local ruler.

The royal families of the pagan English kingdoms would also have had rather more education than the people they ruled over, and they might have been able to understand the Christian message more readily: indeed they might already have heard of Christianity through contacts with other kingdoms. Even if a ruler listened to the missionaries and then turned them away, at least the disappointed Christians might have had the opportunity of making friends at court, and acquiring useful information at a high level.

The disadvantages for Christian missionaries of hob-nobbing with the nobility are just as obvious. Under God, all people are equal, and if you favour a rich and powerful person with the gift of the Gospel first, then you might be said to be neglecting the poor, who are a particular concern of the Christian God. Close links with a local warlord could also lead Christian missionaries into the slimy business of propping up a nasty regime, living the high-life and forgetting basic Christian concerns. As we shall see, Paulinus experienced both the advantages and disadvantages of converting the court, then the country, in that order.

Of the twelve northern saints featured in this book, Paulinus is the one who travelled furthest to get to the North of what we now call England. He was probably Italian by birth, and, like Augustine, had been a monk in Gregory's monastery of St Andrew in Rome, before that famous pope sent him to assist the Christian mission to Kent. This life-changing call pulled Paulinus out of the cloister, put him on the road, and then put him on the sea.

The Anglo-Saxon world Paulinus was to work within would have been as different from the world of St Andrew's Monastery in Rome as lard is from olive oil. The culture of the Anglo-Saxons was in large part a warrior culture – men, and especially kings, were expected to be brave and warlike. The Anglo-Saxon poetry that has survived, including the magnificent epic *Beowulf*, reveals an obsession with battle, arms, plunder and hard drinking.

Writing about the German tribes centuries before some of them came to dominate Britain, the Roman historian Tacitus described how a local ruler guaranteed the love and loyalty of his closest henchmen by giving them rich gifts. Tacitus commented that this method of buying friends meant that rulers had to go on the war-path frequently, so that their supplies of treasure could be replenished.

Tacitus, who knew how much trouble the Germans had caused the Romans militarily, also remarked on their recklessness, indiscipline and all-round lack of professionalism in war. He noticed how peace was regarded by the men of some tribes as an opportunity to sink into drunkenness, leaving them vulnerable to attack.

V. Northumbria

Paulinus and Edwin

In Kent, Paulinus was at least among fellow-Christians, priests and new converts alike; but the marriage of the Kentish Princess Aethelburh to King Edwin of Northumbria meant that he was soon translated to a pagan kingdom in the far North. Paulinus did, however, have a plan to keep him warm: Bede tells us he wanted to be a missionary to Edwin and the Northumbrians, and not just a personal spiritual adviser to Edwin's new wife.

The king of Northumbria had promised to become Christian during the marriage negotiations with his bride's father, but he put off his conversion until an attempt was made on his life in 626, when he had ruled Northumbria for ten years.

The assassination attempt was savage and spectacular, and very nearly successful. An enemy ambassador called Eomer hid a sharp, poisoned knife under his clothes, and lunged forward when Edwin was least expecting it. A nobleman (or 'thane' in the language of the time) called Lilla threw his body into the path of the knife, but the weapon went right through him and penetrated Edwin. Lilla died, but Edwin recovered.

Eomer the assassin had been sent by Cwichelm, king of the West Saxons, against whom Edwin now declared war. He promised to become a Christian if the Christian God helped him defeat Cwichelm, but even after his victory he delayed his baptism, and discussed the matter at length with his closest followers.

According to the *Ecclesiastical History* of the Venerable Bede, one of Edwin's advisers used these discussions to unlock a spectacular metaphor for human life and faith which still has the power to impress us today.

His insight was that human life is like the flight of a sparrow through the great hall of a king, in the middle of winter. To understand this idea, we have to remind ourselves what such a hall was like. In the Anglo-Saxon poem *Beowulf* Heorot, the great hall of King Hrothgar, is repeatedly described and praised for its size and the luxuriousness of its fittings. Heorot has real gold incorporated into its structure, although otherwise its architecture would have been little more sophisticated than that of an elaborate barn. This was where the king fed and watered his picked men, and cemented their attachment to him with many rich gifts, carrying on the tradition described by Tacitus. In return for gifts, land, patronage and other benefits, many of the thanes would have been expected to fight for their lord when the time came.

A series of such great halls, or 'mead-halls' are known to have existed at Yeavering in Northumbria, which was one of King Edwin's residences. The modern equivalent of such a place would be a combination of a throne-room and the banqueting-hall of a great palace.

Many small Anglo-Saxon settlements had modest equivalents of the royal great halls: there is an example at Bede's World in Jarrow, where a few acres of land have been given over to the re-creation of an Anglo-Saxon settlement. As with the royal halls, these were used as places to meet, eat and drink. Smaller houses would be gathered around the great hall, and the whole settlement would usually be enclosed by some sort of defensive wall or earthwork. Anglo-Saxon monasteries, which also needed to be defensible, had their own equivalent of the great hall, in the form of a refectory, which with the monastery church would be one of the monks' two largest buildings. In the early days, the monasteries would have been built from the same modest materials used to shape the buildings of secular communities.

It would have been easy for a sparrow to fly into a great Anglo-Saxon hall, as there would have been no glass in the windows. Even in the depths of winter, some windows would have had to remain open so that smoke from the open hearth could escape. The sparrow, perhaps looking for a place to nest, would fly into the hall and be immediately panicked by the sight of the roaring fire and the roaring Anglo-Saxons who were enjoying its warmth and the hospitality of their sovereign.

What would the thanes in King Edwin's great hall have looked like? Archaeological evidence from Anglo-Saxon graves suggests that they were significantly taller than the Britons they had pushed into the West. They were also taller than the average medieval English person, and in fact any average English person until quite modern times. In the twenty-first century, there are few practical advantages to being tall, but in those days of hand-to-hand combat, Edwin's lanky warriors would have had superior reach, and the ability to deliver crushing downward blows to the heads of their shorter British enemies.

Modern illustrations often show these warlike thanes with full beards, but there is evidence from faces on brooches and other artefacts that they wore large moustaches but no hair on the chin. Victorian history-painters were not afraid to depict men of this period with such moustaches, but this particular type of facial hair can look a little absurd to modern eyes. Militarily, the lonely moustache is, however, a useful tactic as, in the words of Alexander the Great, a beard is just a handle for the enemy.

Archaeology reveals that many Anglo-Saxons had broader tooth-arches than modern people. This means that the gap between their back teeth on the right and left was wider, allowing more horizontal space for the tongue, and for the teeth themselves.

Despite this generous supply of tooth-space, many Anglo-Saxons suffered from overcrowded teeth, still a major source of income for modern dentists and orthodontists. The wide tooth-arch was linked to a low hard palate, which would have made the speaking-voices of these ancient people sound different from the voices of people today.

Anglo-Saxon teeth usually show signs of severe wear, even in cases where the owner of the teeth in question was under twenty years old at death (few Anglo-Saxons lived beyond forty). They also had types of decay in their worn teeth that are unknown in modern times. The excessive erosion of the teeth is now put down to the Anglo-Saxons' coarse diet, much of which would have been made up of bread from flour ground using querns of soft stone. These querns, which were operated by hand, would have left stone-dust in the flour, which in turn would abrade the teeth.

If she was particularly observant, the sparrow flying through the king's hall might have noticed that its human occupants were wearing homespun woollen garments in a variety of colours, held together with brooches and other types of fastenings, some finely-wrought in metals, and good enough to be transferred to a new garment when the old one wore out. Many such fasteners have been found in the graves of these long-dead people.

The image of the sparrow flying through the king's hall in winter is an image of life and death. The unnamed follower of Edwin who gave it voice implied that the howling winter outside the hall was like death itself. His first hearers would have understood only too well how winter could be similar to death.

In northern Europe in the depths of winter much of the vegetation can appear dead, and the lack of food, the effects of opportunistic diseases, and sheer cold killed many people in the night-time of the year. The winters were also harsher then: according to climatologists, seventh-century Northumbria was enduring a very bitter time of it during the reign of Edwin. From around 150 BC to 900 AD the world was a comparatively cold place – in 829 AD a stretch of the River Nile in Egypt froze, so conditions in Northern Europe must have been very harsh. Unlike modern climate change, which is caused by human activity, these fluctuations in the distant past were due to factors such as variations in the heat of the sun, the orbit of the earth, and the activity of volcanoes.

The winter landscape outside Edwin's hall would have been populated by hungry packs of wolves in those days, and although winter military campaigns would have been more difficult to pull off, the danger of armed raids and even full-scale invasions was still ever-present. Seventh-century winter nights in Britain must have had a special terror for those who had to live through them.

The inventor of the image of the sparrow flying through the hall implied that he and his peers knew little about what happened after death. If the Christians can offer us information on this, perhaps we should join them, he suggested.

This implies that the speaker was either ignorant of the old pagan ideas about the after-life, or was already beginning to doubt them. The after-life offered by the northern gods, such as Woden, was imagined as a series of great halls, allotted to various types of dead people. The best-known of these halls of the dead is Valhalla, the warrior's paradise, where those who died well in battle worked their way through an endless supply of pork, washed down with mead milked from a magic goat.

While the man who invented the sparrow metaphor was hoping that Christianity would provide him with reassurances about the after-life, Coifi, another of Edwin's followers, complained about the lack of success his devotion to the pagan gods had brought him. Although he was a pagan priest and had served the gods more faithfully than anyone he knew, yet he had not thrived. Perhaps the old gods had no favours to offer?

It was this same Coifi who later broke the rules of his priestly status by riding a stallion – such men were only supposed to ride mares. He also dishonoured a nearby pagan shrine at Goodmanham in Yorkshire by throwing a spear at it.

Edwin's conversion to Christianity was not entirely based on the advice of his thanes – in fact the bold way his followers spoke in support of the new religion suggests that they already knew his mind was made up, and that the whole discussion with Coifi and the sparrow-man was some sort of ritualised debate.

The king had, after all, lived at the court of the pseudo-Christian monarch Readwald, and it was Readwald who had taken up Edwin's cause and put him on the throne of Northumbria. In the battle against Aethelfrith, Readwald had lost his son Regenhere. Such a sacrifice must have made Edwin see Readwald in a very positive light, and perhaps this light reflected well on the religion that Readwald sort-of followed.

Edwin also remembered an encounter he had had with a mysterious stranger during his time in Readwald's court. According to Paulinus, this stranger had prophesied Edwin's great success as a Christian monarch.

On Easter Day 627 Edwin was baptised at York, the most important city in the kingdom of Deira, along with many of his followers. Baptisms often happened at Easter, which is still regarded as the most important festival in the Christian calendar. Baptism itself was and is seen as a kind of re-birth, and Easter marks the rebirth of Jesus.

VI. Iona and Whithorn

Ninian, Columba and Oswald

While Paulinus was baptising the Northumbrians, Oswald and his brothers Eanfrith and Oswiu, and perhaps four other brothers, were in exile in Ireland, and on the island of Iona. When they arrived at the monastery on this tiny island its founder, St Columba, had been dead and buried for nearly twenty years.

The brothers were on Iona because of the outcome of a war, and the monastery itself owed its origins to the aftermath of a war in Ireland. St Columba was of aristocratic Irish blood, and despite having become a monk and a priest, he had allowed himself to be drawn into a war against a local Irish king called Diarmit.

The war was started by something that wouldn't usually start a war: a book. The book was a compendium of Christian holy books, comprising the Book of Psalms, the first five books of the Old Testament and St Jerome's Latin translation of the Gospels.

This volume was owned by Columba's old mentor, St Finnian of Moville, who allowed his ex-student to read it, but forbade him to copy it. Columba was so taken with the book, however, that he stayed hidden in the church after the last service every night to write out a copy. According to one account, his pet crane kept him company while he scratched away with his goose-quill pen. He didn't need a candle, because his fingers glowed in the dark and illuminated his work. In fact, there are many stories of Columba glowing like a fire-fly at times of spiritual inspiration, or as a sign of his purity and innocence.

Finnian was furious when he found out about Columba's night-time activities, and demanded the copy he had made. The dispute was brought before the local king, Diarmit, at a place called Tara-of-the-Kings in Leinster. Diarmit found against Columba and in favour of Finnian.

Now it was Columba's turn to be furious, and his anger was further stoked up after a youth called Curnan, son of the King of Connacht, sought sanctuary with him. Curnan had killed another young man during a fight at a hurling match (hurling, or 'hurley', is an ancient Irish game resembling field hockey). Diarmit's men failed to respect Columba's church as a sanctuary, dragged Curnan out and killed him.

The resulting battle of Culdreihmne was fought between Columba, reinforced by the army of the King of Connaght; and Diarmit, the supreme ruler of Ireland. During the night before the battle, Columba was visited by the Archangel Michael, who promised him victory – but at a cost. As the army of Columba and the King of Connact advanced the next morning, the archangel was seen leading the troops. Columba's side won, but some three thousand men had been killed. All but one of the casualties were from Diarmit's side.

Unfortunately, any remorse Columba felt about the battle of Culdreihmne did not prevent his getting involved in two further battles on the Irish mainland – the battle of Coleraine, around 579, and the battle of Cuilfedha in 587.

A synod held at Teltown in Meath excommunicated Columba over the Culdreihmne business, but this judgement was soon reversed. Columba was then sent into exile, to any place from which he wouldn't be able to see Ireland. The first island he came to from which his home country could not be seen was Iona. It was here that Columba founded his monastery.

Iona is an island in the Scottish Inner Hebrides, and measures about three and a half miles by a mile. Despite its small size, in Columba's day it eventually came to house about one hundred and fifty monks. Though it certainly served him as a retreat in his later years, Columba had no intention of spending all his time on Iona. Among other schemes, he planned to convert the pagan Picts, whose monarch at the time was King Brude.

The Picts occupied large areas of what we now call Scotland. The Latin name the Romans gave them (from *picti*, meaning 'painted') seems to have had something to do with their habit of either painting or tattooing their faces. The paganism of the Picts was different from the Germanic paganism of the Anglo-Saxons. According to St Adamnan, the biographer of Columba, the pagan priests of the Picts were Druids.

Our main source of information about the Druids is no less an author than Julius Caesar himself. Unfortunately, in his *Gallic Wars* he was writing about the Druids in Gaul and not in the land of the Picts, and he was also writing some centuries before Columba's time. The Druid priests described by Julius are similar in some respects to the later Christian priests. They had a certain amount of political power, and were teachers and guardians of learning. They were also exempt from war-service, and sometimes elected their own leaders, much as Roman Catholic popes are still elected today.

The Druids differed from the Christians in many ways, however, most notably in that, at least in Roman Gaul, they practised both animal and human sacrifice.

Not all the Picts had always been pagan before the coming of Columba. Some of the Southern Picts, who lived in what we would now call the south-west of Scotland, are supposed to have been converted by St Ninian in the fourth or fifth century AD. There is little reliable information about Ninian, but his dates (possibly 360-432?) put him in the last days of Roman Britain. As a young man he is supposed to have travelled to Rome itself, where the pope made him a bishop.

On his way back to Britain, Ninian stopped in Gaul where he met up with St Martin of Tours. Martin had once been a Roman soldier, but had insisted on putting down his sword and taking up the cross. He went on to found the first monasteries in Gaul, and his enthusiastic example inspired Ninian to set up a monastery in Britain. For this purpose, Martin lent Ninian some masons, who were instructed to build him a proper church, of stone. The resulting 'White Church', at Whithorn in Galloway, was perhaps the first Christian church in what is now Scotland.

In his twelfth-century biography of Ninian, Aelred of Rievaulx makes Ninian's mission to the Picts sound like a military campaign planned by an angry warlord:

He didn't like the fact that the Devil, who had been driven under the sea, had still found a safe harbour in a remote corner of this island, in the hearts of the Picts. Ninian therefore armed himself with the shield of faith, the helmet of salvation, the breastplate of love and the sword of the Spirit...

Aelred's biography includes miracles performed by the saint, which seem to have helped him establish himself among both the Picts and the Celts as a sort of Christian wizard. When one of his priests was accused of fathering a child, Ninian persuaded the newborn baby to point out his real father and denounce him, using a deep manly voice and displaying a precocious grasp of Latin grammar.

When Tudwhal, a local king, started giving Ninian a hard time, the saint afflicted him with a terrible illness that made him blind; and also made him repent. Tudwhal's health and his sight were restored when Ninian was convinced that he was truly sorry. Aelred also records how, when reading a book in the open air, Ninian was protected from the rain by a sort of sacred force-field. He was also able to protect his own cattle from rustlers by enclosing them inside another force-field.

Archaeology at Whithorn has revealed evidence of thriving communities there, stretching right back to the middle of the fifth century, but the lack of firm evidence about Ninian makes the outlines of his historical profile blur into Christian legend. Some say that Ninian never actually existed, and that some of the Southern Picts adopted Christianity through contact with their Celtic neighbours to the south. Others theorise that there were two Ninians, who together covered a longer historical period than any one man could stretch to.

Whether any of the Picts were still Christian when Columba launched his mission among their people is unclear. Columba certainly had many adventures in the land of the Picts, including one where he prevented the legendary monster of Loch Ness from eating one of his disciples. On this occasion, Columba and his companions came upon the funeral of a man who had been bitten to death by the Monster. Columba immediately ordered his companion Lugne mocu-Min to swim across the Loch to fetch them a boat in which to cross it. The brave Lugne did so, and Columba was able to restrain the monster as if he had tied him up with invisible ropes.

The Loch Ness story is a reminder that the famous Monster is just one of the alarming monsters, devils and other evil things that Christians thought could be found in pagan lands. These creatures often seem to have been present just so that they could be tamed or killed by Christians, such as Columba or, more famously, St George the dragon-slayer. On his travels in the land of the Picts, Columba also defeated the weather-magic of a Druid wizard, purified a poisonous stream and caused the locked gates of King Brude's citadel to unbolt themselves.

Among the important events that happened on Iona during Columba's time, the 'ordination' of Aidan mac Gabrán as king of Dal Riada around 574 is one of the more important (Dal Riada was a kingdom that spanned north-east Ireland and parts of the west of what we now call Scotland). The fact that King Aidan felt he needed to go through a Christian ceremony, presided over by the abbot of a monastery on a small island, speaks volumes about Columba's prestige and the hold Christianity had over the minds and politics of the Dal Riadans.

When Oswald lived there, the monastery on Iona would have consisted of modest buildings constructed out of planks or wattle-and-daub, huddled inside a defensive rampart, like many towns and villages of the age.

A group of humble buildings surrounded by a defensive wall – this is a description of the monastery on Iona in Oswald's time, and it could also serve as a description of one of the very first Christian monasteries. These were built in the early years of the fourth century in the harsh, dry conditions of the Egyptian desert. St Antony of Egypt, who is sometimes called the founder of Christian monasticism, lived as a solitary hermit until he felt able to accept responsibility for the large numbers of pilgrims who wished to follow him. Soon there were many monasteries in the desert.

Some of Antony's predecessors in the wilderness were Christian refugees from persecution, but many of his successors took to the hot sands even though Christianity was tolerated and even encouraged at home.

It may seem strange that such an important strand of Christian history should have started in what is now a predominantly Muslim country, but in the fourth century Mohammed was yet to be born, and there were many Christians in the Land of the Nile. Thanks in large part to Athanasius's biography of St Antony, the monastic idea spread, and devotees tried to find their own equivalents of the desert on the green hills of Britain and Ireland, or on islands in the sea. These deserts, whether green or yellow, land-locked or surrounded by water, were often said to have been infested with demons before the monks took them over.

The island of Iona was a stronghold of Celtic Christianity, a faith which Columba and his predecessors had brought with them from Ireland. The monks, in their white tunics and leather sandals, studied and worshipped, and also ran the island as a farm. What three, let alone seven, young princes of Bernicia would have found to occupy themselves in such a place is an interesting question.

Dal Riada, where the young princes now found themselves, was a kingdom occupied by the Scots. Although these people later gave their name to the country we call Scotland, they were Irish in origin. Communications with the Irish mainland were good, and Oswald and his brothers are thought to have visited Ireland, and even fought alongside their Celtic hosts in battle.

Oswald himself became fluent in the language of the Scots, and contact with this culture, which had been Christian for some time, began to wean him away from the paganism of his ancestors. His conversion to Christianity cannot, however, have been only a matter of gradual acclimatisation. There must have been something other than mere habit that attracted Oswald to the new faith, as presented to him by the monks, priests and laypeople of Dal Riada.

Oswald's family had been pagan for generations. Very little is known about the Anglo-Saxon paganism of England, so historians tend to rely on what we know of the religion of the Anglo-Saxons' continental ancestors. The sons of Aethelfrith traced their ancestry back to the Germanic war-god, Woden, whose Nordic equivalent was called Odin. Woden seems to have been some sort of ancient king or hero who became a god, as the Roman god Hercules is supposed to have done.

Woden was the centre of a cult which was very well-suited to a warrior culture. Compared to Woden, Jesus Christ, the man/god of the Christians, might have seemed rather insipid. There is nothing to suggest that Jesus was ever in an army or did anything violent, except when he overturned the tables of the money-changers in Jerusalem. After Jesus was arrested, he went to his death like a lamb.

It is impossible to say how much of the Bible or of pagan mythology Oswald would have understood, but by asking the right questions of his monkish companions he might have learned to think of Jesus and the Christian God as far superior to the pagan gods he had been brought up on.

Followers of the gods of the north believed that all the old gods – Woden, Thor, Loki and the rest, would be destroyed and replaced by a new generation of gods when the time of Ragnarok arrived. This Ragnarok or 'twilight of the gods' is one pagan equivalent for the apocalypse described in the last book of the New Testament – the Book of Revelation. One difference between these two apocalypses is that after the Christian version of the end of the world Jesus, God and the saints are expected to be even more powerful.

If Oswald couldn't immediately re-cast his mind into a New Testament shape, tales from the Old Testament might have inspired him more directly, featuring as they do charismatic military leaders such as Saul, David and Joshua. These stories might have given Oswald's pagan warrior brain something familiar to latch onto. He might have been particularly charmed by the story of King David, especially since that king had kept sheep and played on the harp. The Bernicians had their own small, hardy sheep, and enjoyed music from a kind of harp.

Perhaps the mental image of Jesus the monks transmitted to Oswald was not the bearded peacenik version some people identify with today. Although Jesus is sometimes called the Prince of Peace, Christians believe that he fought and won a great battle. Many of the Christian holy men of Oswald's time were thought of as fighting terrific battles, though not with spears and shields. They were engaged in a constant fight against sin and temptation, and against the alarming demons people still believed in. The missionary monks also thought of themselves as waging war against the gods of the pagans they were trying to convert.

There are also some surprising similarities between Woden and Jesus, which would not have been lost on a supposed descendant of the Germanic war-god. Like Jesus, Woden underwent an ordeal when he was fastened to a tree. This torment, which gave Jesus victory over death, is supposed to have given Woden wisdom. Jesus was hanged and pierced in the side, and sacrifices to Woden were also killed in this way. Such similarities between two seemingly very different gods might have meant that the mental leap from paganism to Christianity was not always as long as is sometimes supposed.

The idea of Jesus's sacrifice might have been easier for Oswald to understand than it is for most modern people: Oswald had no doubt attended many ceremonies in pagan temples where animals had been sacrificed to appease Woden or some other god. These sacrifices were supposed to buy something good from the gods – and with his sacrifice, Jesus bought a new age of salvation.

Tacitus gave some details of the religious beliefs and practices of the ancient German tribes from whom the Anglo-Saxons were descended. In a surprising passage in his book *Germania*, he describes how some of the Germans did not make idols to worship, but worshipped unseen gods. This is much closer to Christian practice than idol-worship, even though Christians have been making images of Jesus since very early times.

There is no doubt that Oswald would have spent part of his time on Iona listening to tales about Columba, and the example of this warlike nobleman, who was able to find repentance and deep peace in old age, may have appealed to a young man who knew he had much fighting ahead of him.

It is likely that, during his time in Dal Riada, Oswald got some idea of the power of reading and writing. This was another asset that the Christian monks brought to the table, and the young prince may have been able to understand how an alliance with a highly literate group could improve communications within his kingdom, should he ever manage to recapture it. Reading and writing as practised by the monks of Iona would also have linked this isolated island to places like Rome, and the surviving fragments of its empire.

Oswald is sometimes compared to Constantine the Great, the first emperor of the Romans to encourage Christianity, and it is clear from the stories of Constantine's career that he believed the favouritism he showed to his Christian subjects brought him victory in battle. The idea that Christianity could bring good fortune and a military edge is summed up in an Anglo-Saxon poem about the Bible:

Man, use me well and I will bring to shore
Wisdom and strength, and victory in war.
Make me your hook and I will pull to land

Courage and joy, and friends on every hand.
With my help all your enemies will fall
Before you, and great power will be your haul.

It may be that Oswald came to believe that
Readwald and Edwin had beaten his father because
they had some special advantage conferred on
them by their Christian faith. As Oswald sat on
Iona and thought over the reasons for his exile, he
may have calculated that his chances of re-taking
his kingdom would be improved if he were
baptised first. And of course, it might be easier to
rustle up recruits among the Scots if he shared
their religion.

VII. Hatfield Chase

The Fall of Edwin

Oswald had a long time to wait before his opportunity to regain his father's throne arrived. Edwin reigned for seventeen years, the last six of them as a Christian.

Picking through whatever news came to him during his exile, Oswald might have despaired to learn of Edwin's extending his empire as far west as the Welsh island of Anglesey, and across most of the south, excluding only the kingdom of Kent. If he was of a more optimistic cast of mind, he might have begun to suspect that Edwin was overreaching himself.

Edwin seems to have regularly moved his court between royal residences at Bamburgh, Yeavering and York; as well as places Bede calls Cambodonum and Maelmin, which cannot be identified with any certainty.

It must have been more difficult and dangerous for Edwin to administer his empire from several different places than it would have been if he had stayed put in one palace. It may be that he went to all the trouble of travelling because he felt obliged to show his face and keep the locals loyal.

It is likely that Edwin didn't really govern his empire in the modern sense – the far-flung places he claimed as his own may simply have paid him tribute, or formally acknowledged him as a superior king to their local ruler. The chances are that different places related to Edwin's rule in different ways. In any case, Edwin was widely acknowledged as the *Bretwalda*, the over-king of Britain.

While Edwin was expanding his earthly kingdom, Bishop Paulinus was energetically expanding the number of converts to Christianity in the north and midlands of England. It is said that at Edwin's royal seat of Yeavering Paulinus once spent thirty-six days teaching, and baptising people in the nearby river Glen (in those days it was customary to baptise in running water). In Deira, the southern part of Edwin's Northumbria, Paulinus baptised in the river Swale near Catterick. He also preached and baptised at Cambodonum (perhaps Cleckheaton or Doncaster) and in the kingdom of Lindsey (Lincolnshire).

Perhaps Edwin's power over all these places smoothed the path for the work of Paulinus in a way that a true missionary might have found embarrassing. It may be that powerful people in these regions outwardly converted just to keep themselves in Edwin's good books. Since everybody loves a winner, it is likely that the people Edwin conquered wanted to buy into his whole successful 'brand' by undergoing baptism. If so, then their Christianity may only have been skin-deep, and, like Readwald of East Anglia, they might have continued to honour the old gods as well.

The contrast between a free and sincere conversion, and one that had been influenced by such factors as fear, or hope of worldly gain, seems to have been a live issue at the time. Bede tells us that King Aethelberht of Kent didn't force anyone to convert, but 'showed greater affection for believers'. In stark contrast, in a letter to King Edwin, Pope Gregory counselled him to 'suppress the worship of idols; overthrow their buildings and shrines...'.

Edwin himself won an important prize for the Christian cause when he persuaded Eorpwald, the son of his old ally Readwald, to convert. The fact that Readwald had a son who was still a pagan is more evidence that the East Anglian king took a relaxed approach to religion.

Although Bede says that Edwin brought peace, and what we would now call the rule of law, to large swathes of the British mainland, not everyone was happy about his activities. Cadwallon, the King of Gwynedd in North Wales, seems to have been offended by Edwin's incursions into the far west, and he teamed up with the Mercian pagan prince Penda to make trouble for the King of Northumbria.

Edwin clashed with the forces of Penda and Cadwallon at Hatfield Chase near Doncaster, close to where Edwin and Readwald had defeated Aethelfrith. This area was perhaps an obvious point at which to invade Edwin's southern kingdom of Deira, and one he might have been able to guard more carefully had he not over-extended himself to the south and west.

The defeat of Edwin was pretty convincing, and it allowed Penda and Cadwallon to run riot all over Edwin's kingdoms. Either the victors suspected they could never hold such a large area of land for themselves, or they were motivated by hatred – Cadwallon's hatred of the Angles, and Penda's hatred of the new Christian religion. In any case, the two wrought so much destruction that future chroniclers tried to gloss over this disastrous period and assign it to the reign of King Oswald.

As the first Christian king of Northumbria, and a king who died in battle against Mercian pagans and Welsh heretics (as some might have regarded the British Christians) Edwin was guaranteed the name of saint, although his life does not match up to the more peaceable image of sainthood many hold to today. As a saint he was in any case quickly overshadowed by Oswald, who is much more widely known, and is even regarded by some as the greatest patron saint England never had.

When Edwin fell, Paulinus escaped with the dead king's widow, Aethelburh, her children Eanflaed and Uscfrea, and Aethelburh's grandson

Yffi. He also brought with him some of King Edwin's treasures, including some magnificent church plate. The party managed to reach the comparative safety of the Christian kingdom of Kent. Paulinus remained in Kent, and ended his days as Bishop of Rochester in that county.

Bernicia, the northern part of Northumbria, was now ruled for a time by Eanfrith, who was either a brother or half-brother of Oswald. Since Northumbria had split up again, the southern kingdom of Deira was ruled separately by Osric, a son of one of Edwin's uncles. The defeat of Edwin at the age of forty-nine seems to have discredited the Christian faith. As the Edwin 'brand' collapsed, his replacements turned away from the cross and resumed their pagan practices. But in short order, both of Edwin's successors were killed by Cadwallon.

Osric was killed first. He had been besieging Cadwallon in a fortified town when the King of Gwynedd came out with a huge force. Later, Cadwallon pretended to be making peace with Eanfrith, but killed him and the inadequate guard of twelve thanes that he had brought with him to the peace conference.

The year-long reign of Cadwallon in Northumbria represented a massive setback for both Christianity and the Anglo-Saxon race. Helped by pagan Anglo-Saxons, a Briton had marched out of his own kingdom and regained a huge area of the East. At last, after years of retreat, the Britons had taken their revenge.

The victory at Hatfield Chase was very sweet for Penda as well – Bede tells us that from that year he became monarch of his home kingdom of Mercia.

Bede doesn't tell us what Oswald was doing while Penda and Cadwallon were wreaking havoc in what had once been his father's kingdom. He would probably not have fought alongside Edwin, who had killed his father Aethelfrith, but he may have helped Eanfrith, his older brother or perhaps half-brother.

Of course, if Oswald was fully convinced about Christianity by this time, he might have denied help to Eanfrith if he knew he was soon to turn back to paganism. If Oswald helped Eanfrith in Bernicia at first, then deserted him when he rejected Christianity, Oswald might have returned to Iona just before Eanfrith himself fell.

VIII. Heavenfield

Oswald is Victorious

Oswald met Cadwallon in battle in 635, at a place called Heavenfield, very near Hadrian's wall and eight miles north-east of Hexham.

According to Bede, Cadwallon's forces were much larger, but Oswald somehow managed to defeat them and kill their leader, following a dawn attack. Oswald left no doubt that his army was fighting for the survival of the Anglo-Saxon race in Northumbria, and was also engaged in a sort of religious crusade. He set up a wooden cross before the battle, and rallied his men with prayers.

Adamnan, biographer of Columba, tells us that the Irish saint appeared to Oswald in his sleep before the battle and gave him great encouragement. According to Adamnan, Oswald told his men about this the next morning and they all volunteered to be baptised after the battle. At this time, the Irish biographer tells us, there were only thirteen Christians in the whole of Northumbria – Oswald and twelve followers who had gone with him into exile on Iona.

Adamnan's account contradicts Bede, who

implies that all of Oswald's men were full of Christian zeal. Bede's version could be nearer to the truth, since Oswald's army may have consisted partly of Christians from Dal Riada, and of Anglian soldiers who had converted under Edwin.

Bede and Adamnan, and the ninth-century Welsh scholar Nennius, give us little detail about the battle, but it is possible to speculate about what actually happened on that August day in 635.

It is known that, whereas the Britons had cavalry, the English preferred to fight on foot. The higher-status warriors would travel to the battle (and if possible retreat from it) on horseback, but their steeds were kept well clear of the battle itself. The Welsh *Gododdin* poems, which commemorate a battle between Britons and Anglo-Saxons which happened around 600 AD, give us some details about how the British cavalry would operate.

The horsemen, who resembled the later medieval knights in some ways, wore armour and carried lances. They deliberately trampled over their enemies, so that in the *Gododdin* poems the horses are regularly described as dripping with blood. The tribe of the Gododdin, who are celebrated in the poems, also employed dogs, rather like twentieth-century fox-hunters.

Despite their use of cavalry, the Gododdin (of whom more later) lost the battle described in the *Gododdin* poems – a battle which may have taken place at Catterick in Yorkshire. This may have happened because the Anglo-Saxons at Catterick had walls and trenches around their settlement, which the Britons were unable to penetrate.

Although Bede tells us that Oswald advanced against Cadwallon's forces, it may be that he dug himself in, perhaps on a hill, with Hadrian's Wall at his back. There may have been freshly-made trenches there to slow down the British horses, and perhaps spikes set up in the ground to injure them – the spike technique had been employed centuries earlier by the Ancient Britons against Roman cavalry.

There is mention in the *Gododdin* poems of the use of burning shrubs at the ends of spears. These are described as lighting up a night-battle, but they could also have been used by Oswald's infantry to frighten the horses of the Welsh.

If Cadwallon's cavalry opted to charge uphill at Oswald's position, they might also have encountered arrows. Since the horses would have been slowed down by the hill, riders and mounts would have become fairly easy targets. If any broke through Oswald's defences, they would have been surrounded by foot-soldiers with swords and spears, who could have pulled off the rider and then claimed the horse as their own.

The idea that Oswald dug himself in in this way seems to agree better with the story of his using a large wooden cross placed upright in the earth as his standard. His soldiers would have fought hard to defend this symbol, which would have looked even more powerful on a hill. Perhaps the cross itself was fashioned from two thick wooden poles, originally intended as part of a barrier against the enemy's horses.

If Oswald had managed to engage mounted troops from Dal Riada or elsewhere, his tactics would of course have been quite different.

Oswald's sleeping vision, and his use of an improvised wooden cross as a standard, both link Oswald with the Roman Emperor Constantine. Constantine had a night-time vision of the Christian *chi-ro* sign, which later brought him victory in battle, and was then incorporated into his redesigned standard. This ancient Christian symbol is made from the first two letters of the word 'Christ' in Greek.

The interactions of Oswald, Edwin, Penda and Cadwallon are given something very close to the Hollywood screen-writer's treatment by the twelfth-century Welsh historian, Geoffrey of Monmouth. Geoffrey fills in the gaps of the narrative by making Edwin and Cadwallon into childhood friends, and explains the relationship between Cadwallon and Penda by describing how Cadwallon beat Penda in battle and forced him to become his ally.

Some sources say that Penda fought with Cadwallon against Oswald at Heavenfield, but Bede implies that Cadwallon faced him alone. Bede also suggests that Cadwallon died in the battle – others say he lived to fight another day.

Today, Heavenfield lives up to its name by

being a very peaceful place. There is a small eighteenth-century church with a walled churchyard, and a large wooden cross near the road, put up in 1927. This replaces a stone cross that stood for many years on top of a pagan Roman altar – a symbol of the victory of Christianity over paganism. The Roman wall which, according to some accounts, is supposed to have guarded Oswald's back, exists only in a few fragments at Heavenfield today.

IX. Bamburgh

Oswald and Aidan

For Oswald, his new status as King of Northumbria meant that he could at last return to his father's stronghold of Bamburgh.

The modern Bamburgh castle stands on a rock that rises like a vast aircraft-carrier out of the landscape of the Northumbrian coast. The rock is part of the Great Whin Sill, a geological feature of the north country, formed when lava forced its way through cracks in the earth millions of years ago. When the lava cooled, it formed hard knots of igneous rock underground. Over the millennia, the surrounding rocks were worn away by wind and rain, revealing the Sill. Like Bamburgh, the nearby island of Lindisfarne is an outcrop of the Sill.

The rock at Bamburgh is of an extremely hard black type called dolerite, which is very tough to work. Nevertheless a deep well was dug into this unyielding material in Anglo-Saxon times. It is thought that the well-makers managed this by heating the rock up with fire, then quenching it suddenly with water to make it shatter. It was worth the effort, as a castle with no internal supply of water cannot survive a siege for very long. The twelfth-century historian Simeon of Durham stated that the water from the well was very good.

Today, the rock of Bamburgh is an extremely striking sight, but it must have been even more dramatic in the past. Even in the early nineteenth century, high tide would push the North Sea right up to the bottom of the rock, and it seems that in Oswald's time there was even a small harbour at the north end.

The stone castle complex visitors see today was started in Norman times, and extensively restored in the nineteenth century. The earlier fortress that Oswald would have known was built of wood, but it was by no means the first stronghold on the rock.

Archaeological evidence suggests that Bamburgh, once called by the Celtic name of Din Guayrdi, had been occupied in pre-Roman times by a local tribe called the Votadini. This tribe also had fortresses at Yeavering (later associated with King Edwin) and Edinburgh. They have left an unusually deep footprint on history: Tacitus tells us about some of their battles against the Romans in his book *Agricola*, and they are also commemorated in the aforementioned Welsh poem *The Gododdin* (the Votadini and the Gododdin were one and the same tribe). Unfortunately both the poem and the book relate tales of the defeat of the Votadini.

Bamburgh had been in Oswald's family since the time of his great-grandfather, the Bernician

King Ida. The name Bamburgh may have evolved out of the name Bebbanburgh, which suggests that Oswald's family home had been named after Bebba, his father's first wife.

Archaeology at Bamburgh is still very much a work-in-progress, but the results of recent investigations, combined with the written evidence of Simeon of Durham and the Anglo-Saxon Chronicle, enable us to attempt a tentative description of the rock in the days of Oswald.

There may have been an outer wall of tall, sharp wooden poles right around the edge of the rock. Since these close-set poles could not have been driven into the hard bedrock without a great deal of trouble, they might have formed the outer part of a so-called timber box rampart. Such a rampart would have consisted of an outer and inner wall, the gap between being filled with stones and rubble.

The rampart would have been so heavy that it would not have needed foundations, and it would have been possible for some kind of pavement to be formed out of the top of the rocky in-fill. Thanks to this, guards would have been able to patrol the top of the rampart, to keep a lookout for approaching people, ships or bad weather. In a very windy location like Bamburgh, the heavy rampart would also have served as additional shelter, preventing the buildings inside from being blown down. It would also have prevented children, drunken warriors and sleep-walkers from falling off the rock itself.

Today most visitors enter the castle complex under a wooden portcullis at the south end, but archaeologists suggest that the present St Oswald's Gate at the north end would once have been the main, or even the only, point of entry. This makes sense as the gate would have been near the little harbour, and many people would have travelled to Bamburgh by sea in those days. If an invader managed to get through the north gate, his forces would have had to charge uphill to get to the main part of the settlement inside.

On the top surface of the rock, inside the wooden ramparts, there would have been something like the Anglo-Saxon royal complex that has been investigated at nearby Yeavering. Recent high-tech investigations have revealed what might be the outlines of stone structures built to replace the timber ones Oswald would have known. These would probably have consisted of a great hall, a church, private dwellings, a guest-house, stand-alone kitchens and workshops.

English architecture had not yet reached the stage where different rooms were all bound up in one building. In the early Anglo-Saxon period, each building would have been its own separate room, so that, for instance, food from the kitchen would have to be brought to the great hall via a path outside. The spaces between these highly inflammable buildings would of course have acted as fire-breaks.

There is archaeology to suggest that metal-working was going on on top of the rock. This would have been important not just for making and repairing weapons, helmets, armour and household items, but perhaps also for making magnificent pieces from precious metals, to adorn the king, his thanes, and high-status women. Such fancy items would also have served as gifts to secure the loyalty of friends or potential friends near and far.

As well as the faint outlines of possible buildings, some Anglo-Saxon artefacts have been found during excavations at Bamburgh, including part of a stone chair, weapons, tools, beads, and other jewellery.

Then as now, there was a village nearby, huddled in the shadow of the fortress. In times of war, villagers loyal to the master of the stronghold would have been allowed in, perhaps even with their food, animals and other possessions, leaving an enemy nothing to loot.

Despite the salty, windswept climate of the place, all sorts of plant-life now manages to survive on the steep sides of the rock. It is likely that in Anglo-Saxon times, when a siege was always a possibility, all vegetation would have been regularly stripped off so that attackers could not use the plants as cover, or as a natural ladder to climb up. Something similar was done much later at Durham, where it was illegal to plant trees on the river-banks, as these would have given cover to any invaders.

None of the Anglo-Saxon buildings at Bamburgh would have stretched much above the level of the surrounding wall, but from the wall itself Oswald could have enjoyed views of the Farne Islands while simultaneously listening to the sound of the North Sea lapping against the rocks far below his ramparts.

If the story of the wooden cross at Heavenfield is true, then the new lord of Bamburgh had made a firm statement of his commitment to Christianity – a statement which continued at Heavenfield as it seems the cross was not taken away as a trophy to be displayed in a church or elsewhere. *In situ*, it became a focus of pilgrimage and a holy relic. Fragments of wood from the cross, and even moss scraped from the wood, were said to have healing properties. Oswald's cross-shaped statement had brought him success in battle, so he was encouraged to do more in the Christian direction. His next step was to get help converting all his people to his own faith.

Oswald naturally sent to Iona for a missionary to bring his Northumbrians round to Christianity – the Celtic Christianity of the island was what he knew, and he probably associated the Roman variety with his enemy the late King Edwin. Corman, the first missionary the Iona community sent, was an utter failure. He had to be sent back, because his teaching was too harsh and he found Oswald's subjects crude and intractable.

There is no doubt that there was an element of

culture-shock for Corman, who may never have encountered Angles, or the indulgent life of a royal court, before. On Iona, the monks were supposed to dedicate all their time to serving Christ, even when they were doing such mundane tasks as bringing in the harvest or mucking out the horses. In Oswald's court, those people who regarded themselves as Christians probably managed to be good Christians in church of a Sunday, but would have been hard-drinking warriors some of the time as well.

Some of Oswald's followers were probably still pagans, or had reverted to paganism after the fall of Edwin. The irascible first missionary from Iona would have regarded these 'backsliders' with particular scorn, always supposing that he was able to work out who believed what among these people with whom he would not have shared a common language.

If we assume that there was fault on both sides, then it may be that Oswald and his court just weren't ready for the advent of Corman and his party of monkish brothers from Iona. Perhaps the new king's closest followers had no idea how to treat these humble, plainly-dressed new arrivals with respect.

It is possible that in this and other ways, the failed mission and its unfortunate leader became trapped by the strange paradox of Western Christianity at this time. The paradox lay in the fact that, in many places, the centres of missionary

73

work were monasteries. Although they were often made into bishops, many of the great missionaries of the time had spent some time as monks. As Augustine, Paulinus and others no doubt discovered, the sheltered life of the monastery was very different from the exposed, mobile life of the missionary, especially when some of this life was spent rubbing shoulders with boorish thanes.

Corman may have tried to apply some of the disciplines he had learned in the monastery to life among Oswald's thanes. It was traditional in some monastic orders to give newcomers to the community a hard time, and to frighten them with tales of the hardness and deprivations of the cloistered life. It may be that the leader of the first mission to Oswald's court tried this approach with the residents of the Bamburgh fortress, only to find that it was inappropriate: few if any of them would have wanted to become monks.

The way that many of the missionary monks operated was to take with them a microcosm of their monastery, in the shape of a small group of monks with whom they could live. This was certainly Augustine's approach, and even Gregory the Great had his own coterie of brothers within the Vatican. This would be a way to turn the paradox of life as a missionary monk into a strength, since we know that some extremely active people are often sustained by the islands of peace and rest that they create and maintain in their lives. Returning from a long day negotiating with the barbarian hordes, the prayerful atmosphere of his mini-cloister would, in the modern phrase, have re-charged Gregory's batteries.

It may be that Oswald didn't cater sufficiently for the need of the monks of the first mission to have a place to retreat to. If he built or set aside a house for them on top of the rock at Bamburgh, they would still have been able to see and hear the raucous goings-on at the court of the new king. But when Iona sent him a second missionary, Oswald was better prepared than he had been for the first.

When Corman got back to Iona, a sort of *post-mortem* was held, at which the reasons for the failure of the mission to Oswald's Angles were picked over. Anyone who has ever attended a committee will find something familiar in what happened next. One of the monks stood up and suggested that Corman should have fed the Angles the 'milk of easier doctrines'; that he should have started them off slowly, in other words, and sugared the pill. This monk, whose name was Aidan, had just 'volunteered' himself as Corman's replacement. He was chosen by Ségéne, the then abbot of Iona, to become a bishop and lead the second assault.

We do not know whether Oswald had offered Corman the island of Lindisfarne as the headquarters of his mission, but this place was either offered to or claimed by Aidan. Lindisfarne is just north of Bamburgh on the Northumbrian coast, and Oswald, standing on the walkway at the top of his rampart, would have been able to see the island on reasonably clear days. Bede implies that Aidan himself chose Lindisfarne as his headquarters in Bernicia - if so, Oswald would still have had to have the vision to grant him this semi-island, which his forebears had sometimes used as a last retreat when Bamburgh was overwhelmed by enemy forces.

Today, Lindisfarne is a place of pilgrimage for spiritually-minded travellers. In the last ice age, when a great deal more water was locked up in the ice-caps, and sea-levels were much lower, it was nothing more than an inland hill, used as a camp by hunters. Archaeology has revealed that when the ice receded, the island was used by fishermen, attracted not just by the fish, but by the plentiful shellfish they used as bait. By then it was probably much as it is now: an island connected to the mainland by a causeway, or what geographers call a tombolo, passable only at low tide. This means that the island is, so to speak, semi-detached. The most striking difference between ancient and modern Lindisfarne is the castle that now stands on the dolerite outcrop of Beblowe Crag.

Lindisfarne offered Aidan a more easterly version of Iona, the island where he had previously lived as a monk. It also represented land on which to build a new monastery, and proximity to his patron, King Oswald. The king and the bishop did not, however, have to live in each other's pockets. Especially at high tide, their neighbouring domains were comfortably separated, but if either needed the other, contact was not too difficult.

It must be understood that though Aidan bore the title of bishop, he would not have regarded himself in the same way that Roman Catholic bishops would have at that time. Celtic bishops like Aidan were still very much monks, and as such were under the control of the abbot of their home monastery. Celtic bishops were more like high-status missionaries than the princes of the church that Roman Catholic bishops sometimes became.

When it came to preaching to Oswald's thanes, Aidan's first problem was of course the language barrier. Although he had travelled only a few hundred miles to get to Bernicia, he was at first unable to understand the Germanic language of the Anglo-Saxons, his native tongue being the Celtic language of the Scots. In the early days, Aidan was forced to preach through Oswald, who knew both languages and, it would seem, was able to carry out a simultaneous translation. If Aidan had sufficiently sharp ears, he would probably have picked up some useful bits of Anglo-Saxon when the king translated his words.

The fact that his sermons arrived at the ears of his thanes via Oswald's own mouth must have given Aidan's words a great deal of extra authority, and also a political edge. Any thanes listening to such preaching could not have missed the fact that their new king was anxious to re-establish Christianity in Northumbria, and that he was prepared to go to considerable trouble to do it.

At least some of the thanes at Bamburgh must have been Christians under Edwin, and they might have noticed some subtle differences between the Celtic Christianity that had just arrived from Iona, and the Roman Christianity of Paulinus and Kent. Gregory the Great had made it clear to Augustine that he had no real authority over the Celtic priests, and Augustine's attempts to bring them under the wing of Rome had not been successful. The story goes that Augustine met representatives of the Celtic Church near the river Severn, but that he breached protocol by failing to stand up when they came into the room to negotiate. After that, the negotiations rapidly went downhill. The Celtic Christians of Northumbria were, therefore, a distinct group who were not to come under the authority of the pope until the Synod of Whitby in 663/4.

The Celtic Christians had remained outside the authority of the pope for a long time, partly because of the remoteness of their homeland of Ireland, an island at the extreme north-western edge of Europe, which had never been part of the old Roman Empire. Many other Christian groups lost contact with Rome during the Dark Ages, but the monks Oswald had invited into his kingdom remained independent despite attempts to draw them in, and even though there was now an active Roman Christian presence in Britain.

The Celtic monks shaved their heads differently from those of the Roman persuasion, who shaved the familiar bald patch into the crowns of their heads, so that the remaining hair formed a fringe all round. By contrast, the Celtic monks are thought to have shaved the fronts of their heads, from the forehead up to the crown, and to have left the hair at the back to grow freely.

The organisation of the Celtic Church was based around monasteries, where, as we have seen, the abbots had authority even over any bishops among the monks. This type of organisation was a sacred mirror of the secular hierarchies that governed many small kingdoms in Ireland at the time.

The Celtic Christians had a lot in common with their counterparts among the Romans, including devotion to the Bible and to prayer. The differences between the two approaches were more differences of organisation, emphasis and atmosphere than of doctrine or core values. Although our sources are few, ragged and otherwise imperfect, it would seem that the Celts were more mystical in their religion, and more liable to look to nature as a visible embodiment of spiritual truth.

The Celts were also more given to extremes of fasting and other types of self-mortification than the Romans. Adamnan of Coldingham, for example, only ate and drank on Sundays and Thursdays; and some monks are supposed to have punished themselves by allowing worms to burrow into their skin. The prize for most ascetic Celtic monk must, however, go to one Finnchua of Bri Gobann, who hung from iron hooks for seven years.

This sort of asceticism, or deliberate hard-living, had been inherited by the Celtic Christians from the very first Christian monks. St Antony of Egypt himself is said to have eaten only once every two or four days, and Macarius of Alexandria gave up sleep for so long that he started to go mad, and was forced to abandon the experiment. The same Macarius lived in a mosquito-infested swamp for six months, and underwent such hardship that he was unrecognisable when he emerged.

For Bede, who was an expert in the science of time, a very unfortunate characteristic of the Celtic Christian way was the failure of the monks to calculate the correct day on which to celebrate Easter. As the most important festival in the Christian calendar, it was important to get this right so that Christians throughout the world could celebrate it on the same day. Not surprisingly, however, remote communities such as the Celts had lost track of the latest techniques for arriving at a date for Easter Sunday. The Synod of Whitby resulted in the adoption of the Roman method in Britain, but a really consistent and reliable system was not possible until the introduction of the Gregorian calendar in the sixteenth century.

The date of Easter Sunday still causes confusion in the modern world, since it can fall on any day between March 22nd and April 25th. Calculating it from scratch is very tricky, so that for centuries tables of correct dates for Easter Sunday were copied out and preserved. Such a table appeared in the Church of England *Book of Common Prayer,* first authorised for use in churches in 1549. These tables are among the ancestors of modern calendars and diaries, and are also thought to have been the basis for the *Anglo-Saxon Chronicle,* a record of historical events originally written into the gaps in a table of dates for future Easters.

As the newly-reunited Northumbria began to grow Christian again, Oswald expanded his sphere of influence until, as Bede relates, he ruled more Britons, Picts, Irish and English people than any of his ancestors. As in the case of King Edwin, it is hard to say exactly what types of relationship Oswald maintained with the areas he is supposed to have ruled over. He seems to have established himself as *Bretwalda*, or 'over-king' of Britain, but it is likely that not all of the petty kings of the islands regarded him as their ultimate ruler.

A snapshot of Oswald's status at the peak of his power is provided by Bede's story of his relationship with Cynegils, the king of the West

Saxons. Cynegils had been converted to Christianity by a bishop called Birinus, who had been sent by Pope Honorius I with the modest task of converting any people in Britain who were still pagan. On his arrival, Birinus discovered that the West Saxons, who were also known as the Gewisse, were still entirely pagan, and he decided to concentrate his efforts on them.

When Cynegils was ready to be baptised, Oswald was there to act as his godfather. Later Cynegils became Oswald's father-in-law, when the Northumbrian king married Cynegils' daughter, who may have been called Cyneburh. Together the two kings gave Bishop Birinus the city of Dorchester as the headquarters of his diocese.

This story of a holy alliance between the kingdoms of Northumbria and the Gewisse seems fairly straightforward, but it does give rise to many questions. The first question is, how did Oswald just happen to be in the land of the Gewisse at the precise moment when their king decided to convert to Christianity? It seems likely that the Northumbrian king's presence there was not a happy accident, and that Cynegils was persuaded by both Oswald and Birinus to get baptised. This would have further cemented the links between the kingdoms of Northumbria and the West Saxons - links which may already have been pretty close.

Oswald probably regarded the Gewisse as his allies anyway, since they too had fought against King Penda of Mercia, and against the Britons. It was also Cynegils' son Cwichelm who had sent the assassin who narrowly failed to kill Oswald's rival King Edwin.

Oswald could not, in any case, have just wandered idly into Cynegils' kingdom - so far from home, he would probably have had to be guarded by a small army of thanes and other followers. The fact that Oswald was in what we now call Dorset at all, hundreds of miles away from Northumbria, suggests that his control over his northern kingdom was pretty firm, and that he did not expect to be replaced in a palace coup during his absence.

The trip to Dorset (which was probably more like a state visit) confirms another feature of Oswald's life - that it was full of travel. He had no doubt started life at or near Bamburgh, but then went into exile in Dal Riada and in Ireland proper. He probably came at his enemy Cadwallon from the north-west, and as a king fought battles and forged alliances in the south-west.

The story of Oswald and Cynegils also shows that Oswald wasn't too fussy about what type of Christianity his allies adopted - or perhaps it shows that Birinus, the bishop sent by the pope, had already convinced Cynegils that he should be baptised as a Roman-style Christian before Oswald arrived to act as his godfather.

It would seem that Cynigils' status as a political and military ally, and a fellow Anglo-Saxon, weighed more with Oswald than the denomination the king of the Gewisse had chosen. Presumably, Oswald's tolerance for different versions of Christianity would not have extended to the Christianity of the Britons, such as Cadwallon. Their adherence to their own version of Romano-British Christianity was later taken as a bad mark against them, especially since it seems they never bothered to try to convert the pagan Anglo-Saxon invaders.

While Oswald was spreading his sphere of political influence, Aidan was spreading the Gospel from his base at Lindisfarne. Aidan knew how to lead by example, and his way of life was as inspiring as his preaching, if not more so. He travelled around his new diocese on foot (probably not alone, but attended by some of his fellow-monks), and would approach complete strangers and try to convince them of the truths of the Gospel. If the people he met were already Christians, he would try to strengthen their existing faith.

Aidan took little part in the rowdy high-life of Oswald's royal court, and if he was invited for a meal in the great hall at Bamburgh, he would leave with his monks as soon as possible. The holy men would then return to prayer and study.

When Oswald's visits to Lindisfarne coincided with meal-times, the king would join the monks in a simple meal of bread and water. There is no doubt that the king and the bishop enjoyed a very special relationship, and since Aidan had his own separate little kingdom on Lindisfarne, it seems to have been more a relationship of equals than that between, for instance, a king and his paid chaplain.

To some extent, Aidan was to Oswald what Paulinus had been to Edwin, and it is tempting to compare the Roman and the Celtic bishops. One of the main differences is that, whereas Paulinus was close enough to the then royal family to feel the need to aid the escape of Queen Aethelburh, Aidan was sufficiently semi-detached to be able to continue as a missionary to the whole of Northumbria even after Oswald fell and his kingdom broke in two.

X. Maserfelth

The Fall of Oswald

With Christianity spreading from Kent, Iona, Northumbria and the land of the Gewisse, and with the new religion also pretty well established in East Anglia, it is hardly surprising that the remaining pagan enclaves of Britain were beginning to feel a bit squeezed. Just nine years into Oswald's reign, Penda, the pagan King of Mercia, met the Northumbrian king in battle at a place called Maserfelth, which is traditionally identified as Oswestry in Shropshire.

Bede tells us that this battle was fought between the armies of Penda and Oswald, but given the battle's likely location very near Wales, Penda was probably in some sort of alliance with the Welsh, as he had been when Edwin was killed. In fact, old Welsh sources suggest he fought alongside an army from Powys.

As for the army of Oswald, the majority of the Northumbrian king's forces would have been, in effect, small-time farmers, obliged to serve their local thane, and through him their king, in time of war. They would have been armed with spears, shields, knives and perhaps javelins: a small number of them may also have been archers.

Most of them would have carried spears with them for most of their lives: only a slave was not allowed to carry a spear, and the spear would be broken over his back if he was seen with one. In civilian life, a spear would be a protection against attack by other people and by wild animals – it would also have served as a useful walking-aid during journeys over rough ground. Some Anglo-Saxon spears were specially reinforced so that they could penetrate the round wooden shields of the time.

The Anglo-Saxons called such shields 'lindens' in their own language, which suggests that the best examples were made from lime-wood, a light and strong wood that is easily worked. They might also have associated the lime tree, from which the wood came, with healing, as parts of it are known to have medicinal properties. Archaeology has revealed, however, that not all shields of the period would have been made of lime-wood.

Shields would be covered with leather from a number of different animals - this would have protected the outer surface of the shield from damp. Sometimes the leather was painted, and it is hard to believe that Oswald and his soldiers did not employ some sort of Christian sign such as the *chi-ro* symbol, or a simple cross, or the familiar fish design still used by some Christians.

Archaeology suggests that in Oswald's time

swords were much rarer than spears, and that some of them were superbly made and beautifully decorated, with pattern-welded iron blades and steel edges. Such swords would be cherished and handed down through the generations, and might already have been genuine antiques when they were buried with their last owners.

Some swords were given names, and all sorts of stories would be told about them, as about famous warriors. The hero of *Beowulf* is lent a celebrated sword called Hrunting. Swordsmen would guard against rusty blades by lining their scabbards with unwashed sheepskin. The natural oils that remained in the wool would help the weapon slide out easily.

Only the higher-status warriors would be worth a helmet, and some of these were even more beautifully made and decorated than the swords. The celebrated mask helmet found at Sutton Hoo was probably too fancy for use in battle, but *Beowulf* makes frequent mention of warriors going into battle masked. Like sword-blades, helmets would be made of iron, though the brittleness of this material might have been alleviated by the use of more flexible gold and copper decorations.

In addition to his helmet, Oswald would have worn a mail coat made up of iron rings. Like his helmet and sword, this might also have been a valued heirloom, passed on to him from his father Aethelfrith, perhaps.

It is unlikely that Oswald would have broken

with tradition and fought on horseback. His horse, magnificently accoutred and with an ornate saddle or 'battle-seat' would have remained in the rear. After the battle of Maserfelth, Oswald's horse was never ridden by that king again.

There is no doubt that Penda, Oswald's opponent at Maserfelth, was a formidable war-leader, and the fact that he had already defeated one Christian king of the Angles probably lent confidence to his troops, and sapped the morale of the other side. Penda's success in war must have had something to do with his ability to forge alliances with other princes, and to cooperate with them in attacking a common enemy.

Perhaps Penda found a way to combine the very different styles of fighting of both Anglo-Saxon and British troops to his own advantage. He may have devised some tactical system whereby Anglo-Saxon infantry would be harassed by carefully coordinated waves of British cavalry and Anglo-Saxon foot-soldiers. We can envision Penda calling out orders in both the Anglo-Saxon and the British languages, and springing all sorts of terrifying surprises on the enemy, his fellow Anglo-Saxons.

The Welsh historian Nennius asserts that Penda used 'diabolical agency' to secure success at the battle of Maserfelth. His mention of this reminds us of the fearful belief in the magical powers of the pagans which persisted among Christians at that time.

One might expect that sincere converts to the new faith would have dismissed their old religion as mere superstition, but this was not what happened. The Christians accused the pagans of worshipping demons: a nasty slur on the pagans, but something that also made the Christians fear them. If the pagans made sacrifices to demons, then surely the demons would sometimes feel obliged to help them out. This mindset explains some of the urgency with which paganism was sometimes suppressed.

Before the battle, as Oswald's forces faced Penda's across that stretch of Shropshire land, they might have been able to both see and hear Penda's pagan pre-battle rituals, rituals that many of the Northumbrians might have remembered participating in themselves. Yes, Aidan has told us that Jesus is Lord, they might have thought to themselves; but can he really beat Woden.

At the battle of Maserfelth, Oswald was defeated. It may be this happened because his army was a long way from home, and could not be adequately supplied at such a distance. By contrast, the Welsh were much nearer home, and Penda may have regarded Wales, the home of his long-time allies, as a second home anyway. Penda was also much nearer Mercia than Oswald was to Northumbria.

When Selby Plummer examined what he took to be Oswald's skull at Durham in 1899, he guessed that the massive damage it showed had been caused by a heavy blow to one side, followed by an even more destructive blow to the other side. He guessed that the second blow might have been made even more deadly by the force of gravity: somebody finished Oswald off while he was lying on the ground. The injuries Selby Plummer examined would seem to be consistent with the fatal end of a duel between two swordsmen. Since we do not have Oswald's torso, we cannot substantiate William of Malmesbury's claim that he he died with a small forest of arrows in his breast.

It is said that with his last breath, Oswald prayed for the men he had led into battle. After the battle, when Oswald's retreating troops were probably being cut to pieces by the British cavalry, Penda put the Northumbrian king's head and arms on poles above the battlefield, perhaps as a tribute or offering to Woden.

XI. Bamburgh again

Oswiu becomes King

As Cadwallon had done after the defeat of Edwin, Penda now tried to see how much damage he could do to the Northumbrian Angles, while there was no king to rally them.

From his base on Lindisfarne, Bishop Aidan saw smoke issuing from Bamburgh, and began to pray for the safety of Oswald's fortress. What had happened was that Penda and his troops had dismantled part of the nearby village and piled up its flammable materials against the bottom of the rock, probably at the north-west end. This suggests that Penda had failed to take the fortress by other means, or had quickly realised that fire was the only option. It is to be hoped that look-outs placed on the ramparts of Bamburgh had managed to warn the villagers of the approach of Penda's marauders, in time for them to get inside the fortress, or flee elsewhere.

No doubt Penda's soldiers started the fire with their shields slung across their backs, while the followers of the late king Oswald threw spears, stones and javelins, and fired arrows at them, in an attempt to frustrate their plan. In the event, Aidan's prayers were answered and a change of wind-direction thwarted Penda's attempt at arson.

Unlike the fall of Edwin, the fall of Oswald did not result in the chaotic collapse of his dynasty. The survival of Bernicia, at least, can be put down to the efforts of Oswald's brother Oswiu. Oswiu became king in 642, and ruled for twenty-eight years, nineteen more than his brother. After a year, he felt confident enough to ride to Maserfelth and recover Oswald's head and arms. The head was buried on Lindisfarne, but one of the arms, which seemed to be in a state of miraculous preservation, was displayed as a holy relic in St Peter's Church at Bamburgh. The legend of the 'incorruption' of the arm contributed to the holy reputation of Oswald, and helped him achieve the status of a saint.

The arm was supposed to be incorrupt because it had been blessed by St Aidan. The story goes that when Oswald and Aidan were sitting at dinner at Bamburgh one Easter Sunday, a servant came in and told Oswald that there were some beggars at his door. Oswald sent out all the food that he was just about to eat, together with the silver dish it had been served on, which he ordered to be divided up among the beggars. This could easily have been done at Bamburgh, where archaeologists have discovered evidence of metal-working. Aidan was so delighted with the king's charitable gesture that he blessed the generous hand and arm of the king.

One hundred and fifty years later, the hand was examined by the cleric Alcuin, who found that it was still flexible, and that the finger-nails were still growing.

XII. Gilling, North Yorkshire

The Assassination of Oswine

Although the crown of Bernicia seems to have passed to Oswiu without much trouble, Deira slipped out of the new king's hands. It came under the control of Oswine, a son of King Osric, who had been killed by Cadwallon shortly after he gained the throne of Deira. This Osric was a cousin of Edwin. In the person of Oswine, therefore, Edwin's dynasty was restored, though only for seven years.

Despite the renewed split between the southern and northern parts of Northumbria, Aidan was able to remain bishop of the whole area, and to spend time with the new king of Deira. By all accounts, Oswine was tall and handsome, open-handed and popular. The nature of his relationship with Aidan is revealed in a famous story about a fine horse the king gave the saint to assist his journeys around the kingdom.

Aidan accepted the horse, with its magnificent saddle and tack, but gave it away to the first needy beggar he encountered. When Oswine heard about this, he was furious, but soon made it up with the saint.

Aidan's decision to give the horse away can be interpreted in several different ways. A horse would undoubtedly have been of use to him, especially since he may have been in his forties or even fifties by this time. His habit of going about on foot did, however, put him on the same level as any strangers he happened to encounter on the way, whereas a horse would have put him in a superior position, forced to look down his nose at any pedestrians.

Aidan might have associated a magnificently-saddled horse with warfare, and it was warfare that had robbed him of his great patron, Oswald. Accepting the gift of the horse might also have associated Aidan rather too closely with the Deiran royal house, and as his use of Lindisfarne as his own independent base demonstrates, he didn't want to get too cosy with any of the warlords of the time. Giving the horse away to a beggar might also have directed attention to the plight of the poor in Oswine's kingdom – people who had probably been made poorer by the disastrous effects of war.

When Oswine and Aidan made up their quarrel over the horse, Oswine was surprised to see Aidan crying. In that moment of reconciliation, the saint had seen Oswine's death – a premature death that would come upon the king because he was so much humbler, and altogether better, than all the other kings Aidan could think of.

Oswine met his end at Gilling, near Catterick, in 651. He and his neighbouring king to the north, Oswiu of Bernicia, could never agree, and the armies of the two kings finally faced each other near Catterick. Battle was never joined, either because Oswine's troops fled in the face of superior numbers or, as Bede has it, because Oswine disbanded them when he saw he was outnumbered.

It was now up to the King of Deira to hide himself, but unfortunately he chose the house of a disloyal nobleman called Hunwold. Here Oswine and his thane, Tondhere, were murdered by a local official called Aethelwine. Oswiu's nephew Oethelwald succeeded Oswine as King of Deira.

Oswiu's wife Eanfled was from the royal house of Deira, and was related to Oswine through their great-grandfather Yffi. She persuaded Oswiu to build a monastery at Gilling as a penance for killing her relative.

Aidan lasted only twelve days after the death of Oswine. He died, propped up on the supporting post of a church near Bamburgh, on the last day of August, 651. As the seventeenth century Durham writer Robert Hegge puts it, Aidan thought it a sin to live after so good a king had died. Aidan's head is thought by some to be among those that share a tomb with Cuthbert and Oswald at Durham.

XIII. Melrose and Lindisfarne

Cuthbert

During his life, Aidan helped to inspire and educate a new generation of Christians in his monastery on Lindisfarne, and at the moment of his death he is supposed to have inspired Cuthbert, one of the great stars among the northern saints. In fact, Bede so respected Cuthbert's memory that he wrote a separate book and a long narrative poem about him, as well as including him in his *Ecclesiastical history.*

The story goes that, when Cuthbert was working as a shepherd, he saw and heard a vision of Aidan's soul being lifted up to heaven by angels. This inspired him to travel to the abbey at Melrose, and to become a monk. The shepherd aspect of the story would seem to imply that Cuthbert was a man of humble origins, but the fact that he was raised by a foster-mother, a lady called Kenswith, suggests that he was from an aristocratic family. It was the custom for Anglo-Saxon parents of the more privileged class at this time to farm their children out to foster-parents, rather as some middle-class English parents today pack their children off to boarding schools.

There is an old Irish tradition that Cuthbert was born in Ireland, but his name would suggest Anglo-Saxon rather that Celtic origins.

Having begun with a miraculous vision, Cuthbert's spiritual journey continued to produce miracles, many of which have a rather homely feel about them, because they involve food, and also animals.

On his way to Melrose, Cuthbert had to shelter for a night in a stable, where his own horse uncovered some bread and cheese that were hidden in the roof (the fact that he rode to the monastery on his own horse is further evidence of his wealthy background). Cuthbert shared his dinner with the horse.

When Cuthbert was the monk in charge of the guest-house at Ripon, he went to get fresh bread for a visitor: on his return he found the room full of bread baked in Heaven. The visitor had of course been a angel.

Later Cuthbert and a companion were brought fish to eat by an eagle, and a dolphin grounded itself on the shore so as to serve as a meal for the saint. In line with the self-punishing habits of the Celtic monks, Cuthbert would pray while standing up to his neck in the sea. On one occasion, sea-otters came to dry his feet after one of these bone-chilling prayer sessions.

Plague hit the abbey at Melrose in 664, and carried off Boisil, the prior. This plague would have been of the notorious bubonic variety, against which the Anglo-Saxons would have had little defence, and which carried off many of them during its frequent visitations. We know now that this form of plague is carried from animals to humans by rats, and the people of this time, who lived in close contact with their animals, probably dreaded the plague even more than they dreaded war itself.

Cuthbert succeeded the plague-stricken Boisil as prior, and later filled the same office at Lindisfarne. He could not, however, resist the lure of a nearby rocky island called Inner Farne, where he established himself as a hermit.

Inner Farne lies off the coast just east of Bamburgh, and Cuthbert is supposed to have scared away all the demons that once lived there. Bede's contemporary St Guthlac had the same problem with demons, who had 'great heads, long necks, thin faces, yellow complexions, filthy beards, shaggy ears, wild foreheads, fierce eyes, foul mouths, horses' teeth, throats vomiting flames, twisted jaws, thick lips, strident voices, singed hair, fat cheeks, pigeon breasts, scabby thighs, knotty knees, crooked legs, swollen ankles, splay feet, spreading mouths, raucous cries'. Cuthbert even managed to grow barley to make his own bread on the island, despite sowing it at the wrong time of year.

Cuthbert was not alone in choosing an island for his solitary hermitage, but because of the geography of Britain, not all of its island-hermits were forced to live out at sea. Cuthbert's friend St Herbert lived on the island that was later named after him in the middle of Derwentwater in the Lake District (also known as Owl Island). The aforementioned St Guthlac, an East-Anglian monk, lived in a converted burial-mound in the fens near Cambridge. Cuthbert, Herbert and Guthlac all had to use boats to get to and from their islands.

Although he was not prepared to tolerate demons around his hermitage, Cuthbert was very happy to see eider ducks nesting on it. He even laid down regulations that these birds should not be molested – an early example of conservationist legislation. In honour of Cuthbert, these hardy sea-ducks are known as 'Cuddy ducks' in the north-east.

Although he was far less well-travelled than some of his contemporaries, including in particular the cantankerous St Wilfrid, Cuthbert's life was extremely varied. He was sometimes a hermit, but sometimes also a brave and adventurous preacher who would spend days away from the monastery, preaching in villages and trying to wean the people away from the superstitions that still survived among them from pagan times.

Part of the point of Cuthbert's story is that his long periods of solitude did not drive him mad, or make him unsuited to human company in any other way. Both his solitude and the time he spent among people were part of the larger purpose of his life.

Cuthbert's fame grew the longer he lived at his hermitage, and, thanks in part to a visit from King Ecgfrith, he was persuaded to become bishop of Lindisfarne in March 685. The same Ecgfrith, who had inherited the throne from his father Oswiu, granted valuable lands for the support of Cuthbert's diocese.

Cuthbert died almost exactly two years after he became bishop of Lindisfarne, by which time he had returned to his beloved Inner Farne. His status as a saint was enhanced by the fact that, years later, when the monks on Lindisfarne opened his tomb to recover his bones to use as relics, his body was miraculously preserved.

In later years, the incorrupt body of Cuthbert went on extensive travels until it finally became the reason for the building of successive churches, and at last a Norman Cathedral, at Durham.

XIV. Jarrow

The Venerable Bede

Bede tells us that he was eleven years old when Cuthbert died. By this time, he would already have spent some four years in the monasteries at Wearmouth and Jarrow. He was probably born in north Northumbria, but there is some evidence to suggest that he was somehow related to the kings of Lindsey, an ancient kingdom roughly equivalent to modern Lincolnshire. As a boy, Bede is thought to have survived a disastrous visitation of the plague at Jarrow, which nearly wiped out the entire monastery.

Even in years when the plague didn't come, life in monasteries like Jarrow must have been tough, especially in winter. There are stories of ink freezing in the monks' ink-wells, and the makers of illuminated manuscripts being unable to carry on their marvellous work because they could no longer move their fingers. The wood and wattle-and-daub buildings that typically made up an early Anglo-Saxon monastery must have suffered badly in tough weather, and they were also very susceptible to fire. From the ninth century, monasteries in coastal locations were vulnerable to attack from the Vikings. Of course, many of these drawbacks would also have applied to the secular communities of the time.

The monastic life did, however, have many advantages. The monks were not expected to fight in wars, and, except where they lived with their wives and children, they were able to escape the embrace of family life, which does not suit everyone. Many monasteries enjoyed the protection of powerful local rulers, and were sometimes even headed by members of the ruling dynasties. The monks often lived off the profits from lands donated to them by aristocrats, who wanted to keep the church on their side.

Monasteries were the places to go for a good education in those days, and the literate monks enjoyed contact, through books, with a wider world of history, science, literature and theology. It is no surprise, then, that some powerful people, including kings and courtiers, treated the monasteries as rest homes or retirement homes.

Bede himself dedicated his *Ecclesiastical History* to King Coelwulf, who had given up his crown for a monk's cowl. King Sigeberht of East Anglia also became a monk, but when the kingdom he had given up was invaded by Penda, the pagan king of Mercia, the people dragged him to the battle-field in the hope that he would inspire the East Anglian army. Sigeberht refused to arm himself with anything more than a staff, and was soon killed.

Aristocrats such as Hilda turned the spiritual life into a second career, and other nobles placed their children in monasteries so that they could be monks or nuns for their entire lives. This practice of giving a child to a monastery must have been less heart-breaking in those days, when people had lots of children, but it does seem a little like sacrificing a child to the new Christian God. In any case, these aristocratic 'donated' children frequently ended up as leading figures in the church, since the advantages of their birth often stayed with them.

Not everybody approved of the special treatment children of the nobility received in religious houses. In his *Lives of the Abbots of Wearmouth and Jarrow*, Bede makes it clear that some aristocrats who became monks did not check their noble status at the door, and expected quick advancement and other forms of special treatment. Bede gives us the contrasting example of the seventh-century abbot Eosterwine, who had once been a thane of King Egfrid, but then became a monk of remarkable humility, rolling up his sleeves to help with mundane tasks in the monastery and on its land. On his death-bed, Eosterwine's friend St Benedict Biscop issued a stern warning against the practice of appointing abbots by birth rather than merit.

Although he lived in a place that was very remote from Rome, Constantinople and the

Mediterranean world in general, Bede was probably one of the best-read people in Europe. Despite the costliness of the parchment on which the monks wrote, and from which they read, Bede was able to access learning from all over the known world, and to write extensively on a wide range of subjects, including the Bible, history and time itself. He packed a lot of work into his sixty-two years, and in fact a letter written about his dying days shows him writing, translating, dictating and inspiring his brother monks right up to the end.

Bede's undoubted masterpiece is his *Ecclesiastical History of the English People*, which he wrote in Latin and completed in 731. The book covers nearly eight hundred years of history, stretching right back to Julius Caesar's first visit to Britain in 60 BC. Today, Bede's book exists in numerous different translations, and is still required reading for many students of history and theology.

Although the word *historia* appears in the title, Bede's book is not really a history-book in the modern sense. Bede is not concerned to convey the absolute truth about everything: he wants his history to improve the reader by offering examples of virtue and piety.

The author is not above glossing over things he finds problematic, and cleaning up the dirty details of stories so that they shine a little brighter. Because his main concern is the history of the church, he gives us few details of the English paganism it displaced, although it is clear that he knows quite a bit about this subject. In his book *On the Reckoning of Time* he gives a charming explanation of how and why the pagan English named the months of the year – but the information raises more questions than it answers, and historians have been picking over the bones of the passage for decades.

Bede wears his biases and agendas very much on the sleeves of his metaphorical habit. As a celibate monk living according to the Roman tradition, he is keen to convey the virtues of those who lived as he did. He is also enthusiastic about showing his readers how certain personalities and events in British history mirror those found in the Bible. His fascination with chronology shows up in a concern to link events in the British Isles to contemporary events on the continent: he will sometimes begin an account of some British event with a reminder of who was pope, and who was Roman emperor, at the time.

Bede has a deep admiration for people like Aidan, who was a Celtic Christian, but it is not putting it too strongly to say that he found the Celtic technique of calculating the date of Easter quite abominable. Bede's obsession with the business of dating Easter is one thing that can make his *Ecclesiastical History* a frustrating read. He returns to this question again and again, and the reader has to make an imaginative leap of historical understanding to come to terms with his fascination.

The most charitable way to see this strong thread in Bede's great book is to try to understand that the man from Jarrow, like many modern Christians, wanted to see unity between the various Christian traditions of his time. He was therefore an early champion of ecumenism, as long as this bringing together of the various churches ended up with them all praying inside a Roman church, and singing from the same Roman hymn-sheet.

Uniform observance of Easter, which would have had all Christians celebrating this festival on the same day, would not have guaranteed automatic conformity in all aspects of belief or practice, but, Bede might have said, it would have been a good start.

In writing about groups such as the Celtic, British and Pictish Christians, Bede shows he is aware that these groups were getting Easter wrong partly because, for many years, they had lost all lines of communication with Rome. This type of isolation could of course lead to some strange ideas growing among believers, like weeds in a neglected corner of the garden. In Bede's day, such ideas were called heresies.

A heresy that Bede mentions often is the one started by Pelagius, a Briton born in the middle of the fourth century. Pelagius, who should not be confused with the two popes of the same name, taught against the ideas of original sin, and the need for divine grace to save human beings from hell. Bede regards Pelagius as treacherous and poisonous, and his followers as mad.

Bede saw the potential for closer union with Rome as a guarantee of freedom from dangerous heresies. Once British Christians all became disciples of the pope, new ideas could be exposed to the scrutiny of the religious authorities in the Eternal City, and condemned or commended accordingly. Likewise, exciting new ideas and writings that were approved by the church could travel more easily to the British Isles, if the believers of Britain were in line with believers in the rest of Western Europe.

While he was trying to persuade the races of Britain to embrace the Roman Catholic way, Bede established a reputation throughout the Roman Catholic world that is often under-estimated by modern British people. To give just one example, the fourteenth-century Italian poet Dante, author of the *Divine Comedy*, placed Bede in one of the highest levels of Paradise, eternally dancing around the sun, hand-in-hand with such other worthies as King Solomon, and the sixth-century Roman philosopher Boethius.

XV. Whitby

Wilfrid Takes the Stage

The Easter controversy (also called the Paschal controversy) as it raged between the Celtic and Roman Christians in Britain was finally settled in a place called Strenshall, now known as Whitby. In the plague year 664, when Cuthbert inherited the job of Prior from Boisil of Melrose, an important synod was held there, on the coast of what is now Yorkshire. After some very complex arguments from both sides, King Oswiu of Bernicia smiled and decided in favour of the Roman side. This meant that monks of St Cuthbert's generation had to make the switch from Celtic to Roman practices, and to grow and shave their hair after the style of the Roman tonsure.

Since the kings of both Bernicia and Deira were present, it seems likely that there was a strong political, as well as religious, element to the Synod of Whitby. King Oswiu, who succeeded his brother Oswald as king of Bernicia, had been unable to bring the neighbouring southern kingdom of Deira under his direct control. After the assassination of Oswine, it was ruled by his nephew Oethelwold, who sided with the pagan King Penda of Mercia against Oswiu, his own uncle. When Oswiu finally defeated Penda, probably near Leeds in the winter of 655, his son Alchfrith became the new king of Deira.

The defeat of Penda was probably the most significant military success of Oswiu's reign. This pagan king had been a thorn in the side of the Christian Anglo-Saxons for as many as thirty years. In various battles, he had killed five kings: Edwin and Oswald in the north; and Sigeberht, Ecgric and Anna of East Anglia.

Before his final campaign against the Northumbrians, Penda posed such a threat that Oswiu offered him an enormous bribe to leave his kingdom alone. Penda remained implacable, however, and was not to be bought off, even though by 655 he had married a son and daughter of his own to a daughter and son of Oswiu.

Oswiu's victory over Penda allowed him to place his own son Alchfrith on the throne of Deira, but Alchfrith was not content for long. He began to favour the Roman style of Christianity above Oswiu's Celtic variety, and brought the forceful bishop Wilfrid with him to argue the Roman side at Whitby.

The fact that Oswiu smiled when he agreed to go along with the Roman form of Easter may be because, by agreeing to his son's idea, he was taking the wind out of Alchfrith's sails and avoiding future confrontation. He must have realised that he was also making his own home-life a little more comfortable, as his wife followed the Roman way. This meant that during some fourteen Easters at home in Bernicia, Oswiu had enjoyed the Celtic Easter feast while his wife was fasting for Lent. After the Synod of Whitby, when he embraced the Roman way, every Easter would be like the eight blissful Easters he had spent with his wife when the dates of the Celtic and Roman Easters happened to coincide.

The champion of the Roman way at Whitby was the thirty-year-old Abbot of Ripon, Wilfrid. This son of a Northumbrian thane had already lived on Lindisfarne and travelled to Gaul and Rome before he was called on to speak against the Celtic way at Whitby.

The fact that the Bishop of Northumbria was now going to be based at York rather than Lindisfarne can be seen as another blow against Celtic Christianity. The centres of power for Roman Christianity in Italy, Gaul and elsewhere tended to be based in cities, whereas the Celtic Christians used monasteries as their centres. Sometimes these monasteries were quite remote from large centres of population. This particularly suited Celtic Christianity in the early days in Ireland, as there are not supposed to have been any proper cities there at that time.

The choice of York as Wilfrid's seat looks like an attempt to return to the days of Paulinus, the Roman Christian bishop who had stood at the right hand of Edwin. York had another connection with Rome, as it had been an important base for the Roman army from about 71 to 400 AD. It was there that Constantine, the first Roman Emperor to encourage Christianity, was crowned emperor in 306 AD.

Although he had won a place of great dignity for himself in the city, Wilfrid almost immediately turned his back on his new duties at York. He felt compelled to travel to Gaul to be properly enthroned, since he suspected that too many of the English bishops were Quartodecimans – that is, Christians who were happy to celebrate Easter on the same day that the Jews celebrated the Passover (on the fourteenth of the Jewish month called Nisan). This was quite unacceptable to Wilfrid, and he felt that it invalidated them as bishops. The avoidance or otherwise of a clash between the Jewish and Christian festivals was another dimension to the complex Easter controversy.

Wilfrid didn't return from Gaul for another two years, during which time the impatient King Oswiu had installed Chad as Bishop of Northumbria at York. It took another three years for Theodore, the Archbishop of Canterbury, to remove Chad and replace him with Wilfrid (Chad became Bishop of Lichfield).

Once he had been reinstated as Bishop at York, Wilfrid set about restoring Paulinus's old church in the city, which had become a tumbledown home for pigeons. After nine years as Bishop of

Northumbria, Wilfrid's position was threatened by Archbishop Theodore, who wished to break up his diocese; and by King Ecgfrith, Oswiu's successor, who kicked him out of York. Despite travelling to Rome and returning with letters from the pope written in support of his cause, Wilfrid was imprisoned and then exiled by Ecgfrith. This was the same King Ecgfrith who had persuaded Cuthbert to become Bishop of Lindisfarne.

When Ecgfrith was succeeded by a new king, Aldfrith, Wilfrid was able to return to Northumbria but was later exiled again. Again he went to Rome to appeal to the pope, and was granted a partial restoration of the lands and monasteries he had ruled over.

Wilfrid's character, and his own conception of his role as a bishop, contrasts starkly with what we know of Cuthbert, and earlier saints such as Aidan. As we have seen, the Celtic bishops were more like high-status missionary monks, who operated under the authority of the abbots of their monasteries. Wilfrid was more like one of the Roman Catholic bishops of the later middle ages, who ruled over large dioceses, were personally wealthy and lived like princes. Wilfrid travelled around with a large entourage and was even involved in a minor war when a storm washed his ship up on the land of the pagan South Saxons.

It is clear that Wilfrid got this idea of the proper role of a bishop during his time in Rome and in what is now France. On his travels, he also saw large, elaborate stone churches and abbeys, and he successfully recreated such places back in England.

There is no doubt that Wilfrid was a driven man, and such men are often not the easiest to work with. Whether he was building or restoring a magnificent church, converting the heathen or charming a petty king, Wilfrid was looking for acceptance, but on a very large scale.

The power, wealth and land Wilfrid acquired by befriending the rulers of various small kingdoms clearly alarmed kings like Ecgfrith, who perhaps saw this ambitious bishop as something like a rival king. At times, it seems, the confidence that helped Wilfrid to triumph at the Synod of Whitby shaded into over-confidence and even arrogance.

It may be that Wilfrid appears in a rather negative light in Bede's writings because Bede had once had to clear himself of heresy in Wilfrid's eyes. It seems that in his attempt to establish the right chronology for the whole history of the world, Bede had threatened a long-standing tradition about Jesus, which stated that he had been born at the beginning of the sixth age of the world.

Until Bede wrote his *On the Reckoning of Time* in the early years of the eighth century, many followed Isidore of Seville (c. 560-636) in believing that the five ages preceding Jesus had occupied about five thousand years. Bede calculated that there had been rather less than four thousand years from the creation to the birth of Jesus, which made some readers believe that he thought Jesus had been born at the beginning of the fifth age instead of the sixth.

The accusation of heresy came up under rather embarrassing circumstances. At a dinner in Hexham where Wilfrid was present, a group of monks who had perhaps dined a little too well accused Bede of this heresy of the ages. Bede heard of the accusation from a monk called Plegwin and felt compelled to refute it in his *Letter to Plegwin*. He asked Plegwin himself to deliver the letter to a monk called David, who was supposed to read it aloud to Wilfrid.

XVI. Hilda's Whitby

Caedmon

The Abbey at Whitby, where the famous Synod of Whitby was held, had been built on one of twelve pieces of land promised to the church by King Oswiu, which were granted after he defeated Penda. By promising these estates before the battle, Oswiu no doubt hoped to encourage the church to pray fervently for his victory.

At the time of the synod, the abbey was under the control of an abbess called Hilda, a close relative of Edwin, the first Christian King of Northumbria. Hilda had been baptised by Paulinus on the same day as Edwin and many of his followers - Easter day 627. At the time, Hilda was only thirteen. Twenty years later, having perhaps been married and widowed in the interim, Hilda embraced the religious life and planned to retire to a nunnery on the Continent. Her friend Aidan persuaded her to return to Northumbria, however, and she became abbess of Hartlepool, then later Whitby.

It is interesting to note that, whereas Hilda was baptised as a Roman Christian, and originally planned to live as a nun on the Continent where the

Roman way was more prevalent, yet she was content to follow a suggestion of the Celtic bishop, Aidan. It is possible that Aidan's obvious piety persuaded her to collaborate with the other side in this way: it might also be that she felt there were no sides in the matter, and that a Christian was a Christian, whenever he or she happened to celebrate Easter. In any case, she later sided with the Celtic party against the controversial Wilfrid.

Perhaps because of Hilda's royal connections, Whitby Abbey became an important centre, particularly for Christian education. No less than five of its students later became bishops.

During Hilda's time at Whitby, Caedmon, regarded as the first English poet, discovered his poetic gift. This happened after an event in one of those Anglo-Saxon great halls, where chanting and singing to the harp was an important element of the entertainment. Seeing that a harp was being passed from person to person, and that everyone was expected to both play and sing, the shy Caedmon slipped out and spent the night with the cattle.

In his sleep, a voice asked him to sing. He said he couldn't, but when he tried he found a fine original poem streaming from his lips. It was a song of the creation, and Caedmon went on to become a monk and to compose many religious poems and hymns.

Seven years before her death Hilda was struck down by a fever that gave her great discomfort for the rest of her life. At her death, the monastery bell was rung according to the custom, and it was heard thirteen miles away at Hackness. There, a nun called Begu saw the saint's soul being taken up to heaven by angels, much as a young shepherd called Cuthbert had seen the soul of Aidan rising up nearly thirty years earlier.

The ruins of Whitby Abbey that visitors can see today are the remains of a later abbey than the one Hilda ruled over, but archaeology has revealed traces that are consistent with an Anglo-Saxon settlement and burial ground. These include doughnut-shaped loom-weights, often buried with Anglo-Saxon women, and evidence of glass- and metal-working. Other finds include fragments of Saxon crosses, a perfect little key and a gaming-piece made of the famous Whitby jet.

Archaeology at Whitby suggests that the commanding headland on which the abbey ruins stand was occupied long before Hilda founded her abbey there. The towering cliff-top is not, however, the ideal place for a long-term settlement, as the cliff itself is being eaten away at the rate of about twenty metres per century.

As well as its jet, its status as an ex-whaling port, its monastic history and its link with Bram Stoker's *Dracula*, Whitby is also famous for the fossils found there. These fossilised creatures, such as ammonites, were of course noticed long before Victorian fossil-hunters started collecting and classifying them, and using them in arguments about evolution.

In much the same way that fossilised sea-urchins used to be called fairy bread, ammonites used to be called snake-stones, because the spiral shape of the fossilised shell looks like the curled-up body of a snake. Learned Medieval Christians believed that the world was only a few thousand years old: they could not, therefore, have understood the great age of the fossilised ammonites, or the process of fossilisation. Their explanation was that, just as St Patrick had caused all the snakes of Ireland to die, Hilda had turned all the snakes around Whitby to stone.

Conclusion

A Pattern of Saints

This book has been an attempt to include the lives of twelve of the best-loved northern saints into a single narrative. It has not been difficult to do this, as the lives of these saints are linked in all sorts of ways. St Hilda, for example, was the daughter of a nephew of St Edwin, and was also related to Oswald and Oswine. She was baptised by St Paulinus, and was a good friend of Aidan. As abbess of Whitby, she hosted the famous synod there, where she would have met Wilfrid and perhaps Cuthbert.

The way these saints are linked forms a pattern similar to an Anglo-Saxon knotwork pattern. These complex designs are often found on carved stones of the period, and in the pages of illuminated manuscripts such as the Lindisfarne Gospels. Some even say that the epic Anglo-Saxon poem *Beowulf* has a knotwork pattern similar to the patterns that appeared as decoration on helmets, weapons, jewellery and many other things in Anglo-Saxon times.

The finer examples of this type of knotwork

give an impression of the complexity, inter-connectedness and mystery of creation. Though painted onto two-dimensional surfaces or carved in shallow relief, they create an illusion of depth which serves as a symbol for the partnership of life and belief. The fact that the knots are sometimes formed out of natural subjects, such as the elongated bodies of animals, is a reminder of how the people of this time couldn't help but live close to nature.

The saints featured in this book were also linked by factors other than acquaintance, friendship or ties of blood. Most of them are thought to have come from aristocratic, or at least privileged, backgrounds. Edwin, Oswald, Oswine and Hilda were members of dynasties that ruled Northumbria for generations. Columba was born into the Irish nobility. Wilfrid is thought to have been the son of a minor nobleman, and Ninian, Bede and Cuthbert may have come from similar backgrounds.

The social origins of Aidan and Paulinus are rather more mysterious, but both of them were able to build close relationships with the kings who ruled the lands they were trying to conquer for Christ.

That leaves Caedmon, who might really have been just a humble servant of the abbey at Whitby, until he received his miraculous gift of song.

There are of course factors that set these saints apart from each other. Although they were all bound up with the early history of the Christian church in the north of Britain, the saints were ethnically diverse. Columba and Aidan were Celts; while Edwin, Oswald, Oswine, Bede, Wilfrid and Hilda were Anglo-Saxons. Their Anglo-Saxon ethnicity meant that the ancestors of these saints lived across the sea in what are now Germany, the Netherlands and Denmark. Despite claims that he was of Irish descent, Cuthbert's name suggests that he also was an Anglo-Saxon.

Caedmon is a Celtic name, but the saint spoke and sang in English and lived a long way from the Celtic lands of Ireland and the south-west of Scotland: this tends to suggest that he was an Anglo-Saxon by culture if not ancestry. Paulinus is the most exotic of the bunch, as he was a tall, black-haired Italian with an aquiline nose. Ninian, who belongs to an earlier time, was probably a Roman Briton: a mixture, perhaps, of ancient Celtic and Italian blood.

The twelve northern saints who dominate this book all lived during times of great change, when important decisions had to be made about the future direction of Britain, and the future of the various ethnic groups that lived on these islands.

Ninian lived at the end of imperial Roman domination in Britain, and he took on the task of converting some of Rome's oldest and most implacable enemies. Paulinus came from the new Rome of the popes, and tried to include the English in the new empire of the Catholic church.

Both Ninian and Paulinus were, in their own ways, tackling the eternal problem of how the British Isles are supposed to relate to the Continent of Europe that is only a short boat-trip away.

The resurgence of Celtic Christianity in England under Oswald eventually proved to be a relatively short delay in the process of bringing English Christians under the wing of Rome. Eventually, even Ireland, the home of Columba's Celtic flavour of Christianity, succumbed to the lure of Roman Catholicism.

Edwin and Oswald were both involved in the lengthy and painful process through which, eventually, England became one country under a single monarch. They were also both concerned to maintain the integrity of the English lands in the face of continued assaults by the Welsh.

The consolidation of England, the rivalry between the Celtic and Roman ways, the process of converting the islands to Christianity, and the drift to Rome, all overlapped in terms of chronology. While kings and prelates argued over the niceties of tonsures and the method for determining the correct date of Easter at Whitby, the task of converting all the English from paganism to Christianity was still far from complete.

As the turbulent life of Wilfrid demonstrates, the growth of the power of Catholic Christianity in England presented a bold challenge to the secular power of kings and nobles. The conflict between secular and spiritual powers still persists in Britain, and in many other countries. In the time of Henry VIII, this age-old tussle combined with the king's personal desires and disappointments and led to the English Reformation. It was then that many churches and monasteries founded in Anglo-Saxon times by the likes of Hilda, Columba and Aidan passed into history.

Chronology

410: The Romans leave Britain

c.432: Death of Ninian?

c.521: Birth of Columba

c.540: Birth of Gregory the Great

563: Columba's exile from Ireland

c.586: Birth of Edwin

590: Gregory the Great becomes Pope

597: Augustine arrives in England

601: Paulinus arrives in England

603/4: Birth of Oswald

604: Deaths of Augustine and Gregory the Great

611/12: Birth of Oswiu

614: Birth of Hilda

616: Edwin crowned

627: Edwin and Hilda baptised

633: Death of Edwin

634: Oswald crowned; Aidan comes to Bamburgh? Birth of Wilfred?

c.635: Birth of Cuthbert

642: Death of Oswald; Oswiu crowned

644: Death of Paulinus

651: Deaths of Oswine and Aidan. Cuthbert enters Melrose

655: Death of Penda

c.657: Hilda founds Whitby Abbey

670-80: Death of Caedmon

673/4: Birth of Bede

685: Cuthbert becomes bishop of Lindisfarne

687: Death of Cuthbert

709/10: Death of Wilfrid

731: Bede completes his *Ecclesiastical History*

735: Death of Bede

Further Reading

Bede: *The Ecclesiastical History of the English People,* edited by Judith McClure and Roger Collins, Oxford, 1999

H.R. Ellis Davidson: *Gods and Myths of Northern Europe,* Penguin, 1964

Geoffrey of Monmouth: *The History of the Kings of Britain,* Penguin, 1966

Samantha Glasswell: *The Earliest English: Living and Dying in Anglo-Saxon England,* Tempus, 2002

Seamus Heaney: *Beowulf: A Verse Translation,* edited by Daniel Donoghue, Norton, 2002

Henry Mayr-Harting: *The Coming of Christianity to Anglo-Saxon England,* Batsford, 1991

Clare Stancliffe and Eric Cambridge: *Oswald: Northumbrian King to European Saint,* Paul Watkins, 1995

F.E. Stenton: *Anglo-Saxon England,* Oxford, 1998

J.F. Webb (trans.): *The Age of Bede,* Penguin, 1998

Printed in Great Britain
by Amazon

37467876R00078